What is Emotional Abuse? 15
Is Emotional Abuse a Crime? 22
Cultural Interpretations 24
Coming Over and the Love Fraud 28
The Earning Power & Cultural Conflict 31
Playing the System 42
Are you a Victim? 47
And if you do not believe.. 52
Any Help for Men? 56
Helping the Emotionally Abused Man 60
Coming to Terms and the Aftermath 76
Here and There 82
Looking Forward 86

DEDICATION

DEDICATION

This book is dedicated to all the Men I know and those sadly no longer with us who have suffered domestic emotional abuse. To my Children and to my Family. This work would never have happened without all of them.

O.M. Gansallo.
Walsall. Sept. 2014.
Croydon. April. 2015.
Lagos & Abuja . Sept. 2015/16/17/18

PROLOUGE

If you are reading this page or you want to begin reading this book and you know, you are a bum, Yes, I said it - A Bum. A bum who has many female partners and children scattered all over town and you don't care for their welfare, never support your spouse and children and never have. You are constantly violent towards women, abusive, irresponsible, lazy, living off your 'woman' and not wanting to get a job and making no efforts whatsoever to get a job. Not positive about anything, always drinking, taking drugs and partying without a care in the world when you have responsibilities and you are also physically violent towards your female partner! **This book is not for you.** You need another form of help not covered in these pages.

Most Definitely:

If you are hardworking, always wanting to look after your family, want a family life, have a child/children, and you are always there for them, you take care of them or have done and still want to. If you have a job or searching for a job no matter what it is, so you can support your family, put food on the table, always working so that you can meet up with your mortgage and loans, taking on extra work at every opportunity. No matter what you do, to support your family and according to her, it is never enough?

Does your spouse or partner, constantly put you down, belittles your efforts, and says you are not man enough for her? Does your partner/spouse constantly accuses you of not working hard enough even if you are doing all you can and she sees it, continues to insult your efforts and she contributes little and/or keeps all her finances for herself and nothing you do is good enough for her? If you find yourself feeling low in mood, dreading her next verbal assault, feeling belittled and extremely frustrated and in your mind you ask yourself; 'where am I going wrong?' When you keep on trying and trying to be a good partner and a responsible Father, but she continuously calls you "useless or good for nothing" and she compares you to other men who she says are more successful than you. If you see yourself in these descriptions, then **this book is for you.**

Women aren't the only victims of domestic abuse. One man every three weeks is killed by a violent partner in the UK. A recent survey of over 100 people in Southwark, London, suggested that young men are more likely to accept aggressive behavior from their female partners than women are from their male partners. "Though they almost never report it because it's such a taboo," says domestic violence psychologist Dr David Holmes.

Read on and find out if as a Man, and as a Man from a BME(Black Minority Ethnic) background living in Britain and the Diaspora, you are a victim of Domestic Emotional Abuse from your spouse or partner. Admittedly, while the majority of domestic violence victims heard and recorded and reported are from women, abuse of men happens far more often than you'd probably expect or realise. Typically, men are physically stronger than women but that doesn't necessarily make it easier to escape the violence of the relationship especially if it is emotional. An abused man faces a shortage of resources, skepticism from police, and major legal obstacles, especially when it comes to gaining custody of his child/children or even seeing them, from an abusive mother. No matter your age, occupation, or sexual orientation. Though, you can overcome these challenges and escape the physical abuse and emotional abuse it is still damaging to your well being.

Also when some spouses 'come over' to join their partners, they may be easily influenced and impressionable to bad advice and all sorts of frauds and tricks, that there is a way to get access to money without toil for a chance at a 'better life' without necessary working' Wanting quick easy money for free after a change of status to a British Citizen. Many are approached through their faith groups and are tutored in what they should do. Some of these places aren't really religious. They make friends with people who are not really friends, it could be family members or peer pressure to be like "others" that are seen from the distance as doing well, not knowing their journeys or intent. Some are wrongly advised that it is more lucrative to go it alone and become a 'Single Mum' as long as the children are British Citizens. The priority is no longer to work to keep the family together but to tear the family apart and then the man becomes the bait, used to be constantly reported to the police at whim or always give a threat of calling the police. Then to the law and authorities the man is seen as violent and aggressive on the spouse's word alone, when this is mostly not the truth.
It appears the family laws in the Diaspora are often manipulated by the emotional abuser to justify the plan to have the man (husband/partner) guilty and vilified. This is the same law that is there to protect the innocent and the children, the children are now victims and they become silent witness in this melee. The children are in the middle of it all and a responsible Father would want to avoid this but cannot. In the meantime, so usually, the man is readily branded as the aggressor despite protestations. The current thought is, after all, how can a woman be an aggressor when the man usually is?

There will be false accusations, from your wife/partner, false allegations and pretenses especially when at home behind closed doors and there are no witnesses to see how the verbal abuses and arguments and put downs takes place from your wife/partner. Many of these women are told that British and American authorities protects the 'abused 'mother/woman and children and the authorities will help and support them, signpost them to charities. Friends and family give advice that they can manipulate the system, get access to housing, free money, a stream of benefits, free or heavily subsidized big and new council houses and many more. Many are tempted by the story that they go and do exactly that; work on breaking the man's spirit, undermine the relationship, reporting to police false allegations, building a case, kick the man out of his home, restrict access to the children, and continue to make demands by using the child/children as bargaining tools.

The experience is traumatic and there are no winners. The break up definitely will have a long term effect on the children. And the man in an emotionally abusive relationship often rides a lonely train, he often hides the emotional scars in public as if nothing is wrong and when he gets home, he deals with reality: day in and day out of his emotional abuse. He becomes an expert in living two lives and keeping the secret and remaining silent, he dares not confide in people. Who would believe that the man is the victim of emotional abuse? He lives with the shame if found out, that he cannot keep the family together. All has a serious impact on the emotional and mental health of the abused man.
In the short term, the abuser gets bold and confident, but the long term reality is that cracks will start appearing; children developing behaviourial problems, psychological scars, the burden of being a sole parent, taking sole responsibility and prospect of eventually working one or multiple jobs, being the sole bread winner all begins to kick in.

The Family Laws especially in Britain and America are changing, many are working hard to uncover and reveal the injustice of these abusive acts and, eventually the truth will be out and all the false allegations and playing the system strategies will come to light within these places; where the emotional abuser goes to seek help and support falsely claiming helplessness and victimisation. The time has come for authorities to cotton on to this phenomenon that these people are abusing the system and destroying the lives of their partners and that of their children. The scam to marry a British or foreign citizen and get the citizen status, while ruining the life of the male spouse is real and it is happening up and down these perceived 'milk and honey 'countries and all over the place. Men going through this are ashamed to admit it but it is known in the Black, Multi-Cultural and Ethnic (BME) circles in the Diaspora and has been increasing for years. Is it difficult for most men to admit they have made a mistake that a person they married is now trying to get them out of his property and the country once she has received her permanent residency? Yes it is true, there are women like that!

Read the Chapter 'Coming Over and The Love Fraud'
INTRODUCTION
T

here is a silent, salient abuse which British Men and Men from African/Caribbean Origin suffer in Britain and the Diaspora no one talks about and indeed no one really deeply knows about, what to do

and who to go to and in most cases not even the victims. It is called Domestic Emotional Abuse. This small book will perhaps shock or surprise you but it's intention is to create awareness and begin to try to offer help to those who find themselves in similar situations (which might be you or someone you know!) expressed in these pages to understand what type of help could be offered now and in future. We will have to begin to understand Emotional Abuse and how it affects Men so we may begin to offer appropriate solutions. In future, it is hoped there will be a shelter, a place, a charity, specialist centers, even specific prayer centres in faith groups, in most countries and cities that will offer much needed help to all Men and BME Men.

This book is extended to men and all men from the many cultures and communities (that includes White English and Every Man) that makeup Britain, Africa and the Diaspora who are or have been victims of Domestic Emotional Abuse. However this book concentrates on and gives examples of the effects of this abuse on Black British Men and Men from West African Origin living in the Diaspora. It is not in any way intended to be racist, separatists or misogynist, and in no way whatsoever condones violence of any kind. It in no way deliberately intends to alienate homosexual or transsexual men or women in general. However, it intends to address in particular Men with a wife/partner (even if ex) and particularly Black British Men who are or have been victims of emotional abuse from their spouses who are five times more unlikely to speak about it and seek help. Indeed it is hoped this work will inspire more writings on the subject of emotional abuse from other multi-cultural and relationship perspectives.

This is just one perspective as it is widely accepted if not widely documented that Men from all racial, ethnic, religious and social economical levels and backgrounds in Britain and the Diaspora are also or have also been victims of Domestic Emotional Abuse.

The effects of domestic emotional abuse suffered by men and other men in the Diaspora is not exclusive to only those spouses who commit the 'coming over love fraud' however it is one potent cultural phenomenon that causes this type of abuse. Men form West, East and South Africa living in their respective African countries interviewed for this book also suffer or have suffered domestic emotional abuse. The book to a large extent also concentrates on the cultural ramifications which are not necessarily understood by those who are not familiar with African communities in Britain/America and the deceit of their spouse's 'long game' perpetuated by those who come over to Britain for British passports and citizen status through 'love fraud' for mostly economic reasons. It is clear that those in authority who have never suffered, experienced or even witnessed desperate West African poverty fail to understand the motive of deceptive women brides caught up in poverty 'back home', to gain British status through deception then cry domestic abuse or violence to the British, American and other Courts in the Diaspora.

Finally, this is written as a guide. There will be fine lines to tackle and delicate waters to cross discussing or addressing marriage, partnerships, migration, immigration, cultures and even social class. All written for the quest of understanding and sourcing much needed help for emotionally abused men. Most importantly, it is hoped that this book will begin to help mend fences, build bridges, cerate potential sources of help for men earlier and perhaps save lives.

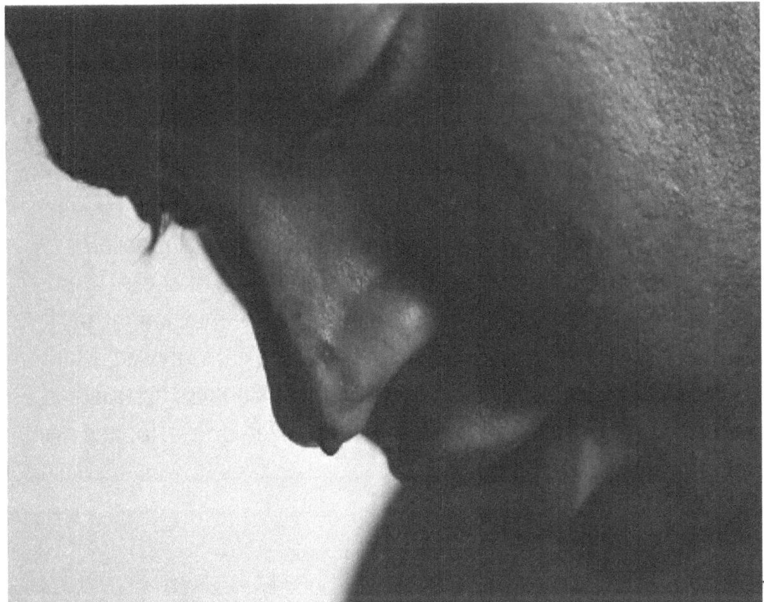

What is Emotional Abuse?

T

here are many definitions of emotional abuse which have varied over the years. Emotional Abuse chips away at a person's feelings of self-worth, confidence and independence. In an emotionally abusive relationship,

the abused person may feel trapped and sees no way out of the relationship or they may feel obligated to stay or they feel walking away may look like failure and that other people will know all about their troubles.

Emotional abuse goes way deep and it is as damaging and traumatic as the physical abuse. It has a long term effect on the person's mental health and well-being. It is systematic, a drip, drip effect that uses mental and passive control of the abuse of emotion to subjugate the person to submission and can after a long term cause more devastating damage on the person the longer the person stays in the relationship. So to have healthy emotions is to be able to react appropriately to the feelings from joy, happiness, frustrations, sadness and anger. So imagine if some of these emotions are shut down one by one so that the abused person does not take joy in any pleasurable pursuits or react to normal emotions and instead, they experience daily put downs , constant verbal abuse, humiliation , feeling bullied, feeling isolated and shame. All these affect the emotional and physical health. So, emotional abuse is a bigger problem than you think and should be taken seriously.

It is important to stress that when most people think of domestic abuse, they immediately think of women being physically abused and assaulted by men. The fact, which many seem to ignore is that not all abusive relationships involve violence and it is not only women who are victims of abuse. Men who are abused are not predominately physically abused, they are mostly emotionally abused and in increasingly cases also physically abused. Many men and women suffer from emotional abuse, which is no less destructive. Unfortunately, male emotional abuse is often minimized or overlooked even by the men being abused.

Understanding Emotional Abuse

The aim of emotional abuse is to chip away at your feelings of self-worth, confidence and independence. If you're the victim of emotional abuse, you may feel that there is no way out of the relationship, or that without your abusive partner you have nothing.

Emotional abuse includes verbal abuse such as yelling, name-calling, blaming, and shaming. Isolation, intimidation, humiliation and controlling behavior also fall under emotional abuse. Additionally, abusers who use emotional or psychological abuse often throw in threats of physical violence or other repercussions if you don't do what they want.

You may think that physical abuse is far worse than emotional abuse, since physical violence can send you to the hospital and leave you with scars. The scars of emotional abuse are very real, though, and they run deep. In fact, emotional abuse can be just as damaging as physical abuse sometimes even more so. Victims can also end up hospitalised.

Most people at some point have been casually emotionally abusive towards someone else, teasing or laughing at others. However at the point when these 'teasing'become personal and intentionally damaging that is when it becomes Emotional Abuse. Many and especially affected men do not recognize this as a form of abuse. As one article states, "The idea that a man could be abused seems unimaginable to many". This is not surprising especially in somewhere like Britain and American research has shown that almost all the images seen and most of the news coverage or accounts on television and the media always portray men being abusive and violent towards women. Also someone who has suffered or is suffering domestic violence, emotional and physical abuse is always portrayed as a woman.

Hardly ever are images seen of women being physically or emotionally abusive towards men. Statistics show that in Britain for example, there are also a growing number of women who are abusive in the same abusive ways towards their husbands and partners and at least one man dies a day from abuse from a female partner. The fact is men do not report this abuse for a abuse from a female partner. The fact is men do not report this abuse for a 65 has risen dramatically over the years. There are a whole lot of presumed reasons why these men would want to take their lives from being naturally ill to losing their jobs etc… However no one asks that why and how does the losing of a job and other emotional aliments caused in relationships with spouses lead men to commit suicide or derail in these times of greater gender and economic equality?

Recognising the Signs of an Abusive Relationship

There are many signs of an abusive relationship. The most telling sign is the constant negative emotional fear of your partner. If you feel like you have to walk on eggshells around your partner constantly watching what you say and do in order to avoid a consistent blow-up by her, chances are your relationship is unhealthy and emotionally abusive. Other signs that you may be in an abusive relationship include a partner who constantly belittles you or tries to passively control you, and lead you to have feelings of self-loathing, helplessness, and desperation.

To determine whether your relationship is abusive, answer the questions below. The more "yes" answers, the more likely it is that you're in an emotional abusive relationship.

Signs that you're in an abusive relationship
Do you:

* Feel afraid of talking to your partner much of the time? * Avoid certain topics out of fear of angering your partner? * Believe that you deserve to be hurt or mistreated?
* Wonder if you're the one who is crazy?
* Feel emotionally numb or helpless?

Your Partner's Belittling Behavior
Does your partner:

* Humiliates or frequently yells at you?
* Criticize you and put you down?
* Treat you so badly that you are embarrassed for your friends or

family to see?
* Ignore or put down your opinions or accomplishments? * Blame you for their own abusive behaviour?
* See you as property or a sex object, rather than as a person?

(Yes! even men are used as sex objects!!)
* Destructive criticism, name calling, sulking constantly when
with you
* Use passive but negative pressure tactics
* Lying to you, or to your friends and family about you
* Persistently putting you down in front of other people
* Never listening or responding to you when you talk
* Isolating you from friends, child/children and family, monitoring
your phone calls, emails, texts and letters.

Below is a real letter sent to an emotional abuser from the abused spouse What could be explored in this letter are the 'incidences' the abused spouse notes down which could signify female–on–male emotional abuse.

Dear............

Again! I will be home soon and hope your usual hatred, maliciousness and spite towards me is not waiting for me. Since you got your precious British passport you have always called the police after creating an argument. You get me arrested and put me in jail for 12 hours, still I have never been charged. You could leave the police out of it this time but it is up to you.

As you know, owing to your frequent police calls on false allegations our children are at risk of being taken into care. So it might help if you think twice before you call them this time at the slightness whim that does not make sense. None of your lies against me will prevail.
When I return home please I ask you not to:

Put my suitcases with my belongings, opened outside in the rain while your suitcases are in the house. I still don't know why you do this
Do not remove my food items from the fridge and throw them in the dustbin for no reason
Do not go into my bags and take my passports or my books, notebooks and throw them in the bin bags outside for reasons I still do not know Do not put my children against me by running with them to school so I cannot walk them to school and telling them not to go anywhere with me Do not spit at me for no reason, trying to provoke me. Please leave me alone Do not hide my tablets from me so I will fall ill when I do not take them. You know I have high blood pressure and diabetes
Do not threaten me. Do not throw clothes at me and shout that you can shout at me anytime
Do not deprive my children of the gifts I brought for them by throwing my gifts away in front of them. You have no right to do so.
Any many more. (All dates of these incidents have been recorded).

You insult me at every opportunity. You show off that you are now studying so you can shout at me and tell me to "piss off" "go and jump in a lake" "you heard me" you are thick" etc.

You proudly show me your fingers to show me you no longer wear my wedding ring, You go out at night to various night clubs without telling me or our children you are going out, you just walk out of the house leaving me with the children and return in the early hours of the morning. I have the dates so do not even think of denying it.

I remember after one of your club nights out. Telling me with defiance and hatred that you can and you will go out when you want!! Thank You! Even your friends know how you treat and disregard me in front of everyone. Go *out as often as you possibly can, enjoy yourself, Catch your Fun. (I have all the dates)! But you have no right to insult me at home after one of your nights out.*

Thanks also for condemning me and calling me a failure. I have no intention of consoling myself. I have accepted my fate. So you condemning me saying "Look at your life" "always stopping and starting" is all good to me. Unfortunately for you we are not still in the village. I use to think couples work together. Sorry in your case I was wrong. All your lies and your false allegations towards me will never succeed because they are all lies. Your attempt to tarnish me as a bad father and a bad husband will never succeed because you and I know it is a lie. I have done more than most fathers you know ever did for their wives and children and you know who they are. Do not try to use my children against me for your own personal deceit and gain. It will not work. No lie can live forever.

As long as you try to make my life a misery by frowning all day and shouting at me and bullying me and calling me brutal condemning names it will not work. God is on my side

As you have said to someone, written in your letter that has stated clearly in black and white that "your (her) goal is to leave her Husband when she is able to....." it is clear you have an intent to leave this marriage since you got your British passport. So you decide.

Our children cannot be exposed to such bitterness and hatred you put towards me for long. So I have a right to also advocate what is right for them. Since you started calling the police as a new British citizen. I have never looked forward again to coming to our home.

All these "your mother your father" abuses which you say regularly is vulgar to me. I am not from that side of the street. I had thought you and many will be beyond that vulgarity by now. Apparently not!

So please let peace be when I return. Leave me alone and do not threaten and bully me. So please think carefully and do what you think best. Enough is enough.
See you soon

With very warm regards for my children
Their Father

This is a true account sent from an emotionally abused man and further evidence and research backed it up. As mentioned before the impact of emotional abuse may be even more devastating than physical assault and have much longer term effects, yet most of the behaviours written in the letter above are not as yet crimes and it is therefore much more difficult to obtain protection, or even to get others to consider them seriously emotionally damaging for the man.

Is Emotional Abuse a Crime?
I

n early to mid-August 2014, the British Prime Minister then announced that discussions were underway in considering making emotional abuse a crime in Britain. Some will be amazed it was not already a crime. In 2018 emotional abused is now a crime.

Domestic violence involving "emotional blackmail" could soon be made legal if a new piece of legislation is passed by parliament. The bill already has support from multiple parties and would make the crime punishable by up to 14 years in prison. The bill has already been passed.

While it's obviously impossible to pinpoint an exact definition of what constitutes emotional blackmail, the bill defines that a man or woman who carries out "a campaign of coercion or intimidation on their partner" would be found guilty of a criminal offense.

The news marks a huge step forward in protecting men and women in the UK against domestic abuse, especially considering it was just last year that the government finally changed the definition of domestic abuse to include emotional, controlling, coercive and threatening behaviour as well as violence. A survey was also taken on a debating television programme in 2014 and subsequently. Almost ninety percent of the British public voted for emotional abuse in Britain to be classed as a crime.

What the survey did not show (which it did not say it would) was how many men called in, in favour and more crucially for this book, how many Black British Men from West African Origin living in Britain were consulted. This we do not know, but it would be fair to assume away from the view of anyone else half of those who called the show in favour were men. The reality and research of course, is that they were probably not and majority of the calls were from women. This is because it is well known that men hardly report physical or emotional and domestic violence from their wives, girlfriends and female partners.

No one, male or female should be constantly emotionally abused, by being shouted at, bullied, ignored, constantly threatened by saying the police will be called out and be made to feel worthless. Men in general feel very embarrassed to admit that they are being bullied, beaten, or abused by their female spouses. With all the universal stereotyping and myths that come with being a man a bold united front is always put up while suffering humiliation behind closed doors. This is even worse for British men from Caribbean and African backgrounds in particular, who suffer most acutely from male stereotyping; big, violent, dangerous and aggressive. When going through emotional abuse men are constantly told to 'man up', 'don't be such a wimp', 'you mean you can't take a bit of banter from a woman? 'What type of man are you'? 'Don't be a big girl's blouse' "Don't be a big softie' and many more of such comments from both men and women. Obviously this does not help and definitely would not encourage men to report all sorts of abuse from their spouses because they want to look tough in front of their friends and look in control of their own lives and relationship in front of their peers.

Then men begin to want to numb the pain and the easiest and best way to do that in that state of mind is to begin drinking a bit too much alcohol and taking a few more drugs which get more lethal, before long both have spiral out of control. Then their problems will be drugs or alcohol or both of which they might get help without discussing where the real problem stemmed from.

Anything will be said as an excuse to start drinking and taking drugs, anything apart from the fact that they are or were being bullied, beaten and emotionally abused by their wives or female partners. For them the shame is too much. Unbearable.

Cultural Interpretations

W

here are the lines drawn in recognising the actual violent Man, BME (Black, Minority, Ethnic) man and the Black British Man of Caribbean and African origin who actually physically abuses his

partner/spouse, beats her up on a regular basis, from the gentle giant from the same cultural backgrounds who believes in 'never hitting a woman' no matter what and has never hit his wife/partner/girlfriend?

How is it established that it is the wife/partner who is emotionally, mentally and in some cases physically abusive towards the man? What are the signs to draw on? How is it determined that she did not intentionally provoke and manipulate the man into a reaction then call the police and fake the situation and claim that it was the man's fault? This is where there are blurred lines and authorities are quick to jump to erroneous conclusion always thinking that the woman is always the victim in almost all abuse cases.

On the flip side, to ignore the woman/wife and her frequent calls to the police is a crime, for it might be true she has been and is being physically abused or abused in other ways. How is it known if it is a true or false allegation, before arresting the presumed accused man and detaining him in a police cell for 12 -24 hours or more?

This is a very sensitive and difficult situation that raises the question of equality and ethnicity from the same ethnicity. Many have said it is easily assumed by the authorities from the police to solicitors that the BME man is automatically presumed to be at fault. There is a perception that a black man is aggressive and dangerous, so little wonder the police, immediately takes the side of the woman shouting false claims and allegations of abuse.

The Black Man does not have a good image in most of the media globally. The covering images of Black Men are that of violent, irresponsible, aggressive, negative attitude, confrontational, drug and alcohol dependent, has numerous partners and children scattered across the city and of course, is a wife/ girlfriend beater. To be honest there are a few who do not do themselves and their communities any favours and their image rubs off on other decent and dedicated Men, Black British Men and other men in the Diaspora. There are bad eggs in all societies and all races but again and again research shows the image of the Black Man is the one constantly trounced with negativity and stereotypes. For those who do not have many or any friends from British African origin, it is astonishing the amount of stereotypes used to describe quintessential 'Black Men' and it is falsely presumed that in parts of the Caribbean and Africa, husbands are allowed to beat their wives and they are easily inclined to do so living in Britain. This is a damaging false general assumption. Domestic Violence and Abuse is NOT accepted in African and Carribean Countries.

The same way that language translators and interpretations are used in different situations dealing with language barriers in multicultural Britain, is also the same way cultural translators and interpretations should be used when dealing with emotional abuse and the conflicts of marriage of different British couples from different cultural backgrounds and ethnic origins living in Britain and the Diaspora.

It has to be questioned why, there is currently a constant occurrence and pattern of false allegations, especially now that there is total positive action and zero tolerance by the police, from many 'British' wives from BME backgrounds and from African/Caribbean origin constantly calling the police for their non-violent innocent husbands, framing him up and giving him an arrest, caution and criminal record, when the truth is that she simply wants to manipulate charities to get free housing and benefits claiming she is suffering from domestic violence, abuse and other ills while she is not.

The question has been frequently asked, that do the authorities simply give these presumed manipulative wives their way because one, it is the Law and they do not want to appear discriminatory, prejudiced or racist, so they immediately accept the wife's false account, two because also subconsciously, it is assumed largely in Britain that the Black Man is naturally aggressive and is automatically prone to beat up and physically assault his wife /partner?

This is when cultural translators and interpretations are needed to assess individual cases and find out if the male or the female in question is actually manipulating the laws of Britain and is actually creating a scene of domestic abuse that is enforced and manipulated because of economic reasons and the fact that financial help, money, grants and free or heavily subsidised accommodation will be provided if they claim to be victims of domestic violence and abuse.

Cultural translators will be able to discern the motives, by understanding the cultural background of these alleged victims without assuming every case is the same, but bear in mind the possibility of the presence of emotional abuse in most cases to the detriment of the man accused. Psychiatrists and Psychologists have to bare this in mind when working with victims of emotional abuse or when the patients presentation is not clear to begin with as it is known men do not admit that they are victims of emotional abuse and it will take a lot of understanding and empathy to get that admission. In future in a multicultural Britain/America, citizens have to be trained in cultural competency as part of being interpreters in a culturally diverse society. It could start from police units. At present many work as language translators but as we are dealing with culture and domestic emotional abuse, studies on cultural translations could be a practical branch of a study in sociology or psychology and practice of social science.

Also doctors, lawyers, social workers, mental health nurses etc… have to work alongside these highly trained cultural translators and also work with these new branches of study to determine, what the motives are of the false allegation of the abuser what the stress factors are of emotional abuse, what the stress sensors are, what the signifiers are. Can emotional abuse be linked to Post Traumatic Stress Disorder? Alcohol, Drug Abuse and Mental Illness of men? Work on this relatively new strand of study must begin now, so as to save the thousands of West African Men, British Men and Black British Men who are being used and abused for their British Passports and who are in need of help but find no one will understand or believe them mostly because they are first Men and secondly Black British Men from different ethnic cultural roots and origins.

There is a presumed reluctance by the authorities in the Diaspora to consider the different cultures of the communities that make up a place like Britain when considering and making judgments on this form of emotional abuse. Having a British Passport does not automatically erase the upbringing from a different country of someone who has got the British passport simply by getting married to a British (or American) Citizen and coming to join their spouse. By being a spouse the person is an adult and it is inevitable that they have formed their own set of values from their home countries. For example getting a British Passport after perhaps 3 years having never been to Britain does not automatically mean the person has or even understands the meaning of British values and cultures.

This can be a thorny issue as it can easily be misconstrued as stoking racism, human rights, multiculturalism, equality and gender rights. However this is where and how the laws of the land can easily be abused and manipulated.

There is a difference between Race and Culture and this is what is to be taken into consideration when endorsing the use of cultural interpreters and translators.

Race is defined as a group of people distinct by their genetic trait within a wider genetic variation, which can be their 'look' 'colour' and human characteristics.

Culture is defined as a people's way of living, how the groups do things collectively and with particular characteristics, which can include a peoples clothing, cooking, music and others.

So speaking about particular cultures that are British in Britain and the Diaspora does not for this book, constitute racism, adverted racism neoracism, the infringement of human rights or gender prejudice.

Coming Over and the Love Fraud
T

housands of Men, British Men from Caribbean/West African origin living in Britain have been victims of the 'she is coming over' syndrome. Finding it quite difficult to build up a lasting relationship

that is not built on perhaps constant partying and clubbing in London or America etc.…, many BME men think they should go 'back home' and 'find' a wife or ask their mothers or family to find them a suitable partner. They too, could be accused of being lost in some romantic idea that a 'girl' from back home will be a good wife because they will have strong belief in 'family values' still much revered in most West African countries by both men and women even now in the 21st Century, and will not be too sophisticated as to not want to cook, or go clubbing and partying all the time. Such hypocrisies are sold to many unsuspecting men by their close family members and even their mothers. Forgetting that the romantic idea of the 'village' good girl who will be a good wife is obsolete and has been thrown out of the window and on to the scrap heap years ago.

However it is important to note that not all men go and 'pick' a 'girl' from home as though they are going to pick a sandwich and bottled water in a supermarket. Many unsuspecting men fall in love with suspecting women who are deceitful and vice versa. Not all or even most men from African/ Caribbean or even Asian communities who are British or American want a 'submissive' wife and partner. There is still the myth that the reason these men went home to get married is because they want submission from their wives, so they went to 'pick' one like picking an object. This is a myth. What about love? and where one finds what he/she might consider love? There is a possibility that many have not been able to find love, companionship or even their soul mate after living abroad for many years. This can and does happen!

Many will tell that the supposedly good wife from 'home' is just as 'sophisticated' as the London/American girl and is probably getting married to you because she wants to get out of 'home' come to London, New York, Paris etc.. and live a 'better life' and do business to make money and more money because the foreign exchange rate is good. This is the Love Fraud. Many will also tell of tales that by the time she 'came over' after being angelic, nice and all the usual clichés of a 'perfect' woman these men fall for, she turned into a 'serpent', 'demon' and removed her 'sheep's clothing' to reveal her true identity as a vicious 'wolf '. Numerous accounts from these men indicate and reveal changes in the 'wife' 'they brought from home' usually occurs when she gets her British/American Passport have children or both.

Their now ex-wives from 'back home' or 'just arrived' usually swear on their mother's, father's, grandfather's, grandmother's, sibling's lives and all the Gods, official and unofficial including all the holy books known to man, that they are not getting married to these men because of their British/American Passport or because they want to come to London, Amsterdam, America, France or any other country with a good global currency etc……. Which of course, is a blatant lie.

So the usually loved up, wet eared, innocent male 'puppies' are on the whole baffled by their wife's from 'back home's' new found attitude and her constant attempts to throw him out of the house or flat he purchased before she 'came over' and her constant 'clubbing, partying, flirting, and to them 'rudeness and lack of respect' (not submission) that would have earned her the reputation as a 'bad, loose girl' and not 'wife material' in her home country. 'Back Home' it is believed her behavior would shame her mother, her family and generally her immediate community.

In some cases many have said their wife now has male lovers to the full knowledge of her husband. In her new found 'free' society she is fully aware her husband can do nothing about her affairs especially when she has set him up to the British law authorities and he has been brandished as a violent, wife beater and even rapist, when she has cleverly played the system and manipulated charities in her favor because she is seen as the 'weaker sex'. Physical violence is never an option and is strenuously not condoned; however it is fair to say such situations can emotionally affect the victim and they can be driven to fits of rage and self-harm. Which again is not condoned but does happen.
In some cases many men have spoken of sitting in front of or passing at a safe distance, the house they once owned when married, and now begin banned from the house and the 'wife from back home' given custody of their children, laughing with pleasure with her new 'man friend 'who has moved in.

As can be imagined many men who have suffered this scenario can suffer acute mental breakdown that can lead them to the church, mosque or asylum and some to the route of drugs and alcohol. In most cases getting to this point has been carefully orchestrated by the former spouse/girlfriend after intensely and purposely provoking her former partner / husband and severely emotionally abusing him sometimes for years.

This is acute emotional abuse which leads to emotional trauma, depression and suicide and not enough is being done to stop innocent men and men of West African Origin living in Britain /America from this brutal treatment.

It is a fact that the mental illness termed Depression leads to suicidal thoughts, attempted suicide and ultimately suicide and a man deprived of this home, property, and child/children is highly venerable to this type of mental illness.

There is a high rate of suicide of Men and Black Men in Britain and America in 2017-19. Unfortunately there is as yet no comprehensive study or research that indicate if these men where in relationships or relationships with female spouses at the time of their suicide.

As mentioned earlier 'coming over and the love fraud' is just one of the triggers that can lead to domestic emotional abuse by deceitful female spouses who come and join their husbands in Britain and America from other perceived less 'privileged' countries for greed not love.

Domestic Emotional Abuse suffered by Men does and still occurs in all relationships regardless of where the husband and wife met and who came over to join who. Men still suffer and are still suffering this form of abuse regardless of their race, culture, social class or sexual orientation.

Also read the Chapter 'Coming To Terms And The Aftermath'
The Earning Power and Cultural Conflict
I

t is well known financial strains in a marriage or in a partnership are one of the main causes of marriage breakdowns. Money is important and crucial however the way money is viewed in a marriage differs in different cultures.

In some African and Caribbean countries the MAN is seen as, and expected to be the main and sole breadwinner in any marriage. He is required to give his wife money to look after her and 'his children' and to 'take care of her' so she can 'maintain herself'; it is viewed as his responsibility. In countries with virtually no welfare many ladies have been known to marry so that they can 'better themselves' and live a 'better life'. So marrying a British foreign Black man is seen as a way out of poverty and a better life anywhere abroad.

This view has been so imbedded in the very fabric of some cultures that it has become the norm for many women to seek to marry a 'rich man'. Many mothers advice their daughters never to marry a poor man. It is widely accepted that this is the same view across the world; however in some West African countries sprinkled with 'big men' it is more glaring. There are sayings in many dialects when translated which states that the beauty of a man is in the size of this pocket. Yes even now when a man wants to woo a woman he has to spend money and the more he spends the more attractive he appears to be. The character and person of the suitor is most times irrelevant as long as he 'has money'. He is expected to continue to keep the woman in the manner that he wooed her. Her family expects it and she demands it. Admittedly, some men go home to marry because they think women from 'home' are unworldly and make fewer demands compared to women in the UK and USA. Time and time again, they have been proved wrong. The blame has to be shared, when some men give the wrong impression that they have means beyond their capabilities when in cold reality, they work so hard for their money and do not have the means to spend as if money was going out of fashion.

Men especially some from some West African countries have been known to want to be 'big men' at all cost for if you have money you have unprecedented access to beautiful ladies and you must be able to look after them, that is giving her money for her to buy all she wants from a new car to shopping trips in London, Paris and America. He is told it is his duty to spend money. So he is expected to spend money to get a wife and (girlfriends). Love as is generally viewed takes on a different dimension. These women actually fall in love with these men first and foremost because they have money. This works both ways and these men are guilty as well of how 'love' is viewed by them when 'picking' a partner. That is the cradle of such love as they know it and where it resides.

Such thinking is usually transported to Britain for example by both British male and female who grew up in certain Caribbean / African countries and find themselves married in Britain. It is forgotten or not understood, that finance is largely an equal effort for both man and wife in a place like Britain and American for instance.

For couples from this cultural framework, when money becomes difficult, change in circumstances, unemployment arrives and all types of financial strains many average families go through, it is easy for the wife to begin to put her husband down, saying he cannot provide for her, his wife, he does not bring enough money home, and he is useless because he may have lost his job. Even if he is trying his best and she hardly contributes financially if she chooses to work, or not working at all. The sole responsibility falls on the man to provide for her the children, now called 'his children' and the household including the rent or mortgage as he did before he became unemployed. He also feels he has let his wife down. The concept of working and struggling together because of love to them is not an option as it is not recognised by these female spouse and partners who complain bitterly if they have to pay just one bill.

When the husband begins to crumble under all these pressures and constant negative` jibes and she also actually mocks him and compares him to rich men 'his mates' etc… he is being emotionally abused. This is just one type of interpretation that is needed to understand 'triggers' that lead to emotional abuse and trauma when dealing with allegations of 'not bringing home enough money home' and gender prejudiced presumed 'male responsibilities'

Acquired mindsets when transported do not automatically or necessarily fit into the society, culture, or country where couples find themselves living. Without understanding the societal framework of particular cultures it is sometimes difficult to adapt and change from upbringing roots. For those with these monetary outlook, it is important for them to understand in the Diaspora not everyone wants to be or can be a millionaire, not everyone wants to be a 'business man' or a corporate high flyer and not everyone wants to drive a Mercedes Benz or BMW car to show off a misplaced sense of wealth because a society and culture like Britain allows the choice to be rich or not to be rich. However both rich and not rich can live comfortably obviously within reason and basic human rights. This is different from not 'having ambitions' or not being 'motivated enough'

In a society where there is welfare, a safety net for all its citizens as opposed to one where there is virtually no welfare, the 'have or die' survival instinct are at opposite ends. Many average, law abiding citizens in Britain can live healthy lives without the need for avarice and the propensity to objectify women as expensive 'things' to be bought with money. For many women who view men and people in general solely by how much money they have, the element of 'poverty mentality' cannot be ignored.

The constant and deliberate flaunting of one's wealth might appear vulgar to many in the British society, while in other societies it is considered normal and even expected. In Britain, the Bus Driver, Postman, Carpenter etc… live in good houses and live good lives, going on holidays with their families in some cases twice or three times a year affordable by collective efforts of man and wife and their jobs.

As many will know, to blame some Black men in the Diaspora for not 'trying hard enough to get a good job' is an injustice. It is difficult and rear for a well-educated Black man in Britain for example to get a job befitting of his qualifications and experience. Highly qualified men from Caribbean/West African origin face immense difficulties owing to all sorts of misconceptions. They are usually labeled as 'overqualified', the position is too 'senior' for them and does not quite 'fit', it is a 'highly sensitive' position and 'trust 'could be an 'issue' etc……… recent research has shown that the Black Woman is 90% more likely to get a senior job than a Black Man in Britain.

For those who do not understand these culture 'battles' and have perhaps never traveled to somewhere like Britain before and come and join their husbands or wives, an explanation is needed for them to understand that Black Men do not automatically get good well-paid jobs in Britain because they are well qualified, the way it happens in their home country. It is not because he is lazy; it is because the dynamics of the society make it difficult. Even when that good well paid job is eventually secured they don't become millionaires over night with money to squander on frivolity.

As mentioned earlier in various communities and especially those from a very strong African base, the man is always looked upon as the sole breadwinner. What now happens if his wife now begins to earn more than him? It is easy for many to view this as irrelevant and to claim that in a country like Britain where being a 'house husband' and a 'new man' are now widely accepted it has not always been so. Britain in the 1950s to the 1980s was also within the societal fabric of the man being the bread winner. Equal pay for men and women has been rigorously reviewed over the last 30 years and is still being discussed now.

The British Ministerial Cabinet has only recently made a positive drive to include more women in the cabinet. In America, 'God's Own Country', where the American dream is for all to succeed without discrimination of race, gender or sexuality and equality for all, American has never had a Woman President only recently in April 2015 has the former first lady and secretary of state Hilary Clinton put in her bid to run for the office of president in 2016.

Imagine now certain cultural roots where the woman is considered as someone to be taken care of by her husband and the wife expects the husband to take care of her and her children at all costs (misplaced as it may seem)

Then imagine now coming to Britain or America and after studying and working, she now begins to earn more than her husband and the position of breadwinner is shifted. Both husband and wife who are not used to this new concept have to be aware that they do not begin to emotionally abuse each other the effects of which could lead to drastic circumstances. Counseling and preparation is needed for this to be recognised and addressed quickly.

The wife with her new earning power and her newly found freedom can easily begin to abuse such power as she will begin to see her husband as inferior, not needed and not 'pulling his weight' in the family in most cases forgetting that he was the one who supported her through her settlement and sponsored her education when she first 'came over'. She now feels she is in the position of control and adopts a superiority complex to the extent that she begins to emotionally, verbally and in some cases physically abuse her husband. Research has shown this stems from a 'poverty mentality' complex. She is now earning as much as or far more than her husband and as far as she is concerned this is her time to put him down and in certain cases to purposely emotionally abuse him.

The husband on the other hand begins to feel inferior and could easily fall into 'I am no longer a man' syndrome carrying on his shoulders all the pressure of what his society and community have thrown on his shoulder of what constitutes a 'man' and a 'good husband'. A consciousness of being useless and unworthy sets in fueled by the constant 'put down' from his wife, a thriving ground for domestic emotional abuse.

When there is a strong love and partnership orientated outlook whether there are children involved or not it does not matter who earns more money than the other the husband or the wife. This is not to say the shift in earning power from wife to husband and vice versa cannot create conflict. However this should be recognised and discussed at an early stage to avoid emotional abuse. This is where the question could be asked; what was their spouse's motive for partnership or marriage initially, love or fraud?

With the full permission of the author, here are some of the examples in America which reports a combination of 'Coming Over, The Love Fraud' and Earning Power & Cultural Conflict citing the extreme emotional and mental effects it can have on Men written by: ABIODUN LADEPO

ABIODUN LADEPO JAN 22, 2014.
An Epidemic: Nigerian Men Killing Their Nurse Wives in the US.

"Yes I have killed the woman that messed up my life; the woman that has destroyed me. I am at Shalom West. My name is David and I am all yours."Those were David Ochola's words during his 911 (U.S.Emergency Number) call to authorities after shooting dead his 28 years old wife, Priscilla Ochola, in Hennepin, Minnesota. The 50-years old husband was tired of being "disrespected" by his wife, a Registered Nurse (RN) whom he had brought from Nigeria and sponsored through nursing school only to have her make much more than him in salary - a situation which led to Mrs. Ochola "coming and going as she chooses without regard for her husband." The couple had two children – four year old boy and a three year old girl. In Texas, Babajide Okeowo had been separated from his wife, Funke Okeowo, with whom he resided at theirDallas home. Upon the divorce, the husband lost the house to his wife, along with most of the contents therein, as is usually the tradition in U.S. divorces where the couple still has underage children.

Mr. Okeowo, 48, divorced his wife because not long after she became a RN and made more money than him, she "took control" of the family finances and "controlled "her husband's expenditure and movement. The husband

could no longer make any meaningful contribution to his family back in Nigeria unless the wife "approved" it. He could not go out without her permission. Frustrated that his formerly malleable wife had suddenly become such a "terror" to him to the point of asking for in court and getting virtually everything for which he had worked since coming to the US thirty years prior, the husband got in his vehicle and drove a few hundred miles to Dallas to settle the score. He found her in her SUV, adorned in full Nigerian attire on her way to the birthday bash organized in her honour. She had turned 46 on that day. Mr. Okeowo fired several rounds into his wife's torso while she sat at the steering wheel, mercilessly killing her in broad daylight.

Also in Dallas (they sure need anger management classes in Dallas), Moses Egharevba, 45, did not even bother to get a gun. The husband of Grace Egharevba35, bludgeoned her to death with a sledge hammer while their seven years old daughter watched and screamed for peace. Mrs. Egharevba's "sin" was that she became a RN and started to make more money than her husband. This led to her "financial liberation" from a supposedly tight-fisted husband who had not only brought her from Nigeria, but had also funded her nursing school education. Like Moses Egharevba, Christopher Ndubuisi of Garland, Texas, (these Texas people!) also did not bother to get a gun. He crept into the bedroom where his wife, Christiana, was sleeping and, with several blows of the sledge hammer, crushed her head. Two years before Christiana was killed, her mother, who had been visiting from Nigeria, was found dead in the bathtub under circumstances believed to be suspicious. Of course, Christiana was a RN whose income dwarfed that of her husband as soon as she graduated from nursing school.

The husband believed that his role as a husband and head of the household had been usurped by his wife. Mr. Ndubuisi's several entreaties to his wife's family to intercede and bring Christiana back under his control had all failed.

If circumstances surrounding the death of Christiana's mother were suspicious, those surrounding the death of a Tennessee woman's mother were not. Agnes Nwodo,a RN, lived in squalor before her husband, Godfrey Nwodo, rescued her and brought her to the US. He enrolled her in nursing school right away. Upon qualifying as a RN, Mrs. Nwodo assumed "full control" of the household. She brought her mother to live with them against her husband's wishes. Mrs. Nwodoquickly familiarized herself with US Family Laws and took full advantage of them. Each time the couple argued, the police forced the husband to leave the house whether he had a place to sleep or not.

On many occasions, Mr. Nwodo spent days in police cells. Upon divorcing his wife, Mr. Nwodo lost to his wife the house he had owned for almost 20 years before he married her. He also lost custody of their three children to her, with the court awarding him only periodic visitation rights. Even seeing the children during visitation was always a hassle as the wife would "arrive late to the neutral meeting place and leave early with impunity."Mr. Nwodo endured so many embarrassing moments from his wife and her mother until he could take it no more. One day, he bought himself a shotgun and killed both his wife and her mother.

Caleb Onwudike's wife, Chinyere Onwudike, 36, became a RN and no longer saw the need to be controlled by her husband. Mr. Onwudike, 41, worked two jobs to send his wife to her dream school upon bringing her to the US from Nigeria. After four years, she qualified as RN. Once she started to make more money than her husband, she began to "call the shots" at home. She "overruled" her husband on the size and cost of the house they purchased in Burtonsville, Maryland. She began to build a house solely in her name in their native Umuahia town of Abia State, Nigeria, without her husband's input whatsoever. Mrs. Onwudike came and went "as she liked," within the US and outside the US. In fact, she once travelled to Nigeria for three weeks "Without her husband's permission" to lavishly bury her father despite her husband's protestations that they had better things to do with the money. Mrs. Onwudikel et her husband know that this was mostly her money and she would spend it however she wanted. Through her hard work, she had risen to a managerial position at the medical center where she worked. Upon her return from burying her father, her husband got one of her kitchen knives and carved her up like Thanksgiving turkey inside their home on New Year's Day.

Death is death no matter how it comes. But the goriest of these maniacal killings is probably the one that happened here in Los Angeles, California. Joseph Mbu, 50, was tired of his RN wife's "serial disrespect" of him.

The disrespect began as soon as she became a RN. Gloria Mbu, 40, had once told her husband he must be "smoking crack cocaine" if he thought he could tell her what to do with her money now that she made more money than him. Before she became a RN, Mr. Mbu had been very strict with family finances and was borderline dictatorial in his dealings with Mrs. Mbu.

However, Mrs. Mbu learned the American system and would no longer allow any man to "put her down." When Joseph Mbu could not take it anymore, he subdued his wife one day, tied her to his vehicle and dragged her on paved roads all around Los Angeles until her head split in many pieces.

[Author's note: Although these are true stories, all the names and some of the details of the incidents have been altered as a mark of respect to the families involved. All of the killer husbands noted in these stories were found guilty. Most of them received the death sentence. Only the California and Maryland culprits received life sentences without the possibility of parole.]

It often comes to some Nigerian men living in the US as a rude shock when their wives become the household's bread winner. Having been accustomed to the docility, domestication, subjugation and outright terrorization of women back home in Nigeria, many Nigerian men are astounded when their wives assert their financial, behavioural and social independence. It is commonplace for Nigerian men to take important family decisions without consulting their wives; to travel out of town and indeed out of country without consulting their wives. Some do not even bother to inform their wives! It is not a big deal for Nigerian husbands to answer phone calls from their girlfriends while lying in bed with their wives; to buy expensive gifts for their girlfriends 'and making only perfunctory, casual attempt to conceal such gifts. It is nothing strange for Nigerian men to, in fact, bring those girlfriends to their matrimonial homes while their wives are home! Some Nigerian men think they have the carte blanche to do what they want because they are the bread winners. What's the wife going to do to them? Beat them? Leave them? Leave them after one, two or three children? Who's going to marry her? So some Nigerian men think. This cruel and phenomenal hostage-taking by Nigerian men in Nigeria is what Nigerian women in America are trying to stop. And they figured out the easiest way to begin curtailing these bullish husbands' wings is to improve their own potential to earn more.

A good way to earn a decent pay in the US (unlike in Nigeria) is to become a Registered Nurse. According to the US Bureau of Labour Statistics (BLS), the median annual salaries of RNs, based on information from May 2012, is $68, 000, while the mean annual salary is $69,000. The middle50% of RNs earns between $54,000 and $78,000. Only10% of RNs earns less than $44,000, while some 10%earns more than $97,000. The BLS also reports average hourly wages: The median hourly wage of a RN is$32.00 and the mean hourly wage is $33.00. The middle 50% of RNs earns wages of $27.00 to $40.00, with 10% of them earning less than $22.00 while 10%earns more than $48.00 an hour.

Some Nigerian men in the US are quick to send their "newly-imported" wives to these nursing schools in the hope that once the women graduate, they (the husbands) could take control of their finances and continue their enslavement. You can imagine a man who was probably a menial worker earning less than$30,000 annually in an expensive place like California or New York going back to Nigeria to "oppress" the village with dollars. He finds a "village girl," brings her to the US and sends her to nursing school. When she graduates and makes twice his salary, he begins to feel inferior to her and his macho instincts take control of him, catapulting his emotions over his sense of reason. If the RN wife decides to take a second or third job, she can easily triple or quadruple the gap between her earnings and those of her menial job husband's. Working long hours takes the wife away from home and because nurses are expected to work overnight shifts, you end up with a husband who is usually home alone at night with just the children. Since even "normal "marriages can be potentially stressful endeavors, adding spousal jealousy and a husband who sleeps alone half of the time to the equation will certainly test the limits of the marriage.

It is the reason why even when such husbands do not go over the hill to kill their wives, they divorce them in epidemic numbers. A friend in New York told me that RN women there are being divorced in droves as if they are plagues.
What is the big deal if a RN wife makes more money than her husband? There are several other professions in which wives make more money than their husbands. In fact, I know of a few military couples with the wives senior in rank to their husbands even though they joined the military at the same

time. Yet, nobody is killing or divorcing anybody. Is this strictly a RN thing?

It is not clear if this is strictly a RN (Registered Nurse) thing, however in Britain there is a growing trend of some nurses replicating the same domestic emotional abuse patterns described by Abiodun Ladepo. In fact, almost 60 percent of the Men of African and Caribbean origin living in the Diaspora interviewed for this book said their ex-wives are nurses who they 'brought over' from African/Caribbean countries and in most cases sponsored their studies directly or indirectly to become nurses.

It is hoped that Britain and other countries in the Diaspora will not go as far as the American Dread (not dream) stated above. Still there is a growing concern that if this 'epidemic'is not carefully and lawfully handled now, the consequences for all will be regrettable and devastating.

Also read the Chapter 'Here and There'.
Playing the System
R

ecently, many unsuspecting individuals, groups and organisations that have been spoken to during research for this book have been amazed at the amount of cases seen and heard of women from

different Caribbean, African and in particular West African countries marrying African British/American men and then abandoning them at the convenient time, usually when they have got their foriengPassport, most especially when they have two or more children from their marriage to a Citizen abroad and become financially independent. This is just another form of illegal immigration and can be termed 'married illegal immigration' and even 'legal illegal immigration'. Mainly it is a marriage of convenience for the emotional abuser.

As this book is being written, it has been heard in the media over 20 men, women and children were found in the container of a ship and one man died, Also that Calais has threatened to close its border to Britain because of the immigrants that try daily to get into Britain and another ship container filled with immigrants was found with yet more human hopefuls trying to enter

Britain, France, Germany and numerous other countries for a 'better life' The Libyan' Neo Black Slave Trade' crisis and many other stories and reports in the media. Year after year the immigration crisis gets deeper, more complicated and depressing.

This is how many women who fake love marry citizens abroad and those who are British from African Origin for becoming British and gaining a British Passport and coming to Britain in deception to find a 'better life' and not for love or indeed marriage. The same trend is rampant in America. So it applies for most of these manipulative 'wives' that when they do get their much craved British or American Passport they begin to try to do away with their spouse, as he/she has served their purpose. One of the quickest and easiest way to do that is to fake being a battered wife! and accuse their innocent husband/partner of domestic abuse. In some cases this deception also applies to passport and citizen seeking husbands. However it is usually passport and citizen seeking wives with children who are more prone to this deception using emotional abuse to their end because the 'system' makes it easy for them.

There is a carefully calculated system to playing the legal and charity organisations which are perpetuated and tapped into by those who 'advise' women in some British/American churches' and communities. When she begins to call the police frequently anytime you have a minor disagreement, she is building a dossier for you with authorities and a case for later, so when she finally applies for benefits from a charity, financial welfare and divorce proceedings, it will be on record that she has called the police numerous times for your 'unreasonable behavior' or verbal 'abuse' which she might have actually started. if no one bothers to check how lame or fickle the calls out were on paper the Judge will simply see you as a violent thug and grant her, her deceitful wishes not knowing it was all premeditated.

Many stories are abound of the wife that purposely tears out her clothes and cuts herself with a knife and then calls the police saying that her husband/partner has been physically violent towards her. Many stories of women being brutally physical towards their husbands and then daring him to touch her in retaliation. Many who call the police on phone shouting that their husband is beating them as they call only for other phone recordings to show the complete opposite. These images and accounts of false allegations are on the internet. yet little or nothing is done to bring these women to justice especially if they have a child or children As the law stands in Britain you will be immediately arrested and charged before an investigation begins. It is her word against yours and the police will go for her word. The man is mostly always to blame. As research has shown If you are a Black Man you are initially likely never to be believed that you are innocent. And your spouse knows that! So she plays the system to her advantage.

It is also quite disturbing that without your knowledge or anyone asking for both sides of the story after an allegation a wife can get a non-molestation and occupancy order against you, termed 'without the respondent being present' (when you have actually not molested her and there is no evidence) but when she gets this without your knowledge and she calls the police, the police are likely to arrest you without question. (The power of arrest).

You can be arrested and will be asked to leave your home for months a year or more and told not to come near your home simply because you are the man! You can be arrested and banned from your own home even if you have lived there for 50 years and you brought the home into the marriage before an investigation by the police and the courts.
These actions in place for real abused women are usually abused by the fraudulent complainant, a right she knows she can use to spite, upset, charge and displace her husband/partner. Even though the police will say that they can arrest the wife if the husband reports verbal or physical abuse towards him, the fact is that this is very rare and if there are children involved the move to arrest the wife is usually delayed or not enforced because she is the woman and she is seen as the main care giver of the cild/children. Cases have shown that many in this situation have been asked what the husband did to provoke the wife. A question that is almost never asked is, if the woman provoked the man because of an obscure notion that the woman is 'the weaker sex'a notion that is constantly flaunted, misused and manipulated by the women who play the system.

It is emphasised again that trained cultural translators and interpreters are needed at all levels and in family mediation. resolution and mediation. Solicitors could also take an extra course on cultural translation so they are equipped to also provide this service to spot and cull false allegation against innocent men.

Husband and Wife might be from the same cultural background living in Britain and the Diaspora but expectations of what is expected of each other and how that differs in the country of where they now live as man and wife should be understood, discussed and clarified. Putting everyone in the same basket and treating them blankly as man and wife full stop, at the courts, with solicitors, by the police, and at mediation, fails to address and resolve the cultural challenges that currently occur to manipulate protective laws. It is not sufficient to assume, think and define all women from all cultures as prone to be submissive, angelic and victims of 'Men'.

So often it has been recorded and witnessed that the manipulative trait of the emotional abuser is to always play the victim when they are the ones really victimising and emotionally abusing. The abuser is always quick to say to all that the person they are abusing is the one that actually needs help when the reality is that is very far from the truth. The worrying problem is almost all will believe her as 'we' have been programmed to always think the MAN as a villain that has to be caged. Even men are quick to turn against fellow men in these instances without taking time to assess the situation and accusation. Stop, Look, Listen and Learn. Before immediately judging.
It is important for all (especially men) to know how many women 'play the system' in Domestic Abuse cases. For those who do not know, the Family Law Courts are different from the Criminal Law Courts and all laws are always changing. It is advised that you get yourself conversant as much as you can with the protective laws for women and children in Britain, America and the Diaspora. This can be accessed by the information from friends and family Lawyers (if you know one) and Lawyers can be expensive. Do not rely on assumptions. What you think might seem ridiculous to you is actually the Law in some countries. What you might consider unfair and unjust is actually fair and just to the law in some of these countries. Many women have played the 'system' and got away with their deceit and they continue to do so and get away with all little or large wealth the man has endured to build over years by deceitfully playing the victim. For example divorce affects inheritance so your heirloom that has remained in your family for over 50 to 100 years can be affected and split to her advantage once you are married and have children. It does not matter if you married in another country the Laws

of Britain and America still considers both or you as married if you live together and have children in their country.

As a Father you are not considered the main care giver to and for your children unless in extreme circumstances. Your children will automatically be given to your ex-wife or partner to care for and you could be systematically removed from your children's lives when you have done nothing to them! Children are the immediate bait of the female emotional abuser as the family courts are geared around the protection of children. By using children they have a winning ticket to emotional use and abuse the man.
According to many men, even though you have been spat at, kicked and violently hit by your female partner if you 'touch' her and I mean 'touch' not hit and even try to restrain her vicious blows (which is not advocated in any way) in self defense and she calls the police you as the man will be arrested and prosecuted not her. If there is an argument and both of you exchange hurtful words if she calls the police you will be charged with domestic abuse.

The use and mention of ABUSE and VIOLENCE is the buzzword and keyword for the domestic emotional abuser and she uses it all the time and at any junction to the detriment of the man. Even some family lawyers tell their emotional abusive clients that the law is on their side and they are encouraged to brutalise the man and claim all types of abuse constantly abusing the abusive laws.

The laws that were written and are in place to protect women from drug addicts, alcoholics, potential murderers and the mentally ill among others are now served to all regardless and the emotional abuser knows this and 'plays the system' to her advantage as a woman and to your disadvantage as a man. Men are advised to protect themselves and be on guard even in the personal walls of your home and rooms. As a man you can be falsely accused of all sorts and almost no one will believe you because you are a man.

This is what some domestic emotional abusers know and what they are taught to become domestic emotional abusers when they commit the love fraud and come 'over' to the 'west' from other countries.

Some deeply held traditions concerning marriage in some countries in West Africa taught to both men and women of their 'roles' are completely shattered when they live as a married couple in Britain, because the 'customs and culture concerning marriage are completely different.

Also read the Chapter, Any Help for Men?
Are you a Victim of Domestic Emotional Abuse?
1. Has she begun to constantly pick arguments with you at random and for no apparent reason?
2. Do you find yourself scared to come to your home when she is in to avoid another row?
3. Does she constantly snap at you and reply you with sarcastic answers to simple questions and is always verbally abusing you?

4. Has she begun to constantly fling your belongings away with disgust?
5. Does she constantly put you down and make you feel worthless?

6. Has she begun to slowly separate herself and her belongings from you?
7. Does she put you down in front of her friends and in front of your friends?

8. Have you lost your job, currently unemployed and she taunts you, laughs at you and constantly calls you jobless and useless? Even if you are gainfully employed, or actively seeking re-employment?

9. Has she begun to throw objects at you and begin to smash up your surroundings?

10. Does she compare you to other men and say they are more successful than you are and you are not meeting up to her wants, needs and standards?

11. Do you think she has severe mood swings and does not want to talk to you about them?

12. Has she began to go out at night with her friends, without telling you where she is going, returning in the early hours of the morning and gets angry with you when you ask her where she has been?

13. As she began to refuse to go anywhere with you and (your child/ children, if you have any) so that you deliberately do not have any family outings?

14. Are the only times she actually speaks to you is when she demands money from you?
15. Does she constantly walk out on you mid conversation when you are trying to communicate with her for understanding and peace?

16. Have you heard her constantly talking about you on the phone with disgust and laughing at you with disdain to one or more of her friends deliberately within your earshot?

17. Has she refused to consummate your marriage in any romantic way? 18. Does she tell you she has had better lovers with more prowess's than you?
19. Do you feel she is always provoking you to lose your temper and frustrate you?

20. Has she stopped telling you where she is going or where she is coming from and walks in and out of the home at all hours of the night?

21. Does she frequently dress up all sexily then goes out clubbing and partying at night without saying a word to you returning the next day or 48 hours later saying you have no right to question her even if married?

22. Has she deliberately and constantly thrown your food away as she has now stopped cooking for you and you have also stopped cooking for her?

23. If you have child/children does she dominate them and influence them not to take the gifts you buy them or eat the food you cook for them?

24. Do you feel she constantly takes her anger and frustrations out on you and bully you?
25. When you have disagreements after she has verbally abused you for days, weeks and hours, does she always threaten to call the police (This is also bullying?)

26. Has she thrown or started to throw harmful objects at you such as plates, cutlery and even Clothes? (This is domestic violence. Go to the Police and report the incident).

27. Has she spat directly at you, on your face or any part of your person?

(This is also domestic violence. Go straight to the Police report the incident and get them to take a DNA of the spittle on your person or your clothes as evidence).

28. If you have a child/children, does she regularly take them away for the weekend or for days, weeks and hours without telling you where your child/children are? (This is against the Law; you have equal rights to your children and the right to equal parenting. She has no right not to inform you of their whereabouts even if you are both still in disagreement).

29. Do you feel and are you convinced you have been used and abused and unfairly treated?

30. Do you feel you have done all you can to work at your relationship but she is not willing in any way to communicate and work with you?

If you answer YES to just 3 of these questions you are at risk of being emotionally abused.
If you answer Yes to 9 of these questions you are being emotionally abused.
If you answer Yes to over 15 of these questions you are being severely emotionally abused.

Those are just some of the pointers, towards being emotionally abused there are many more. It will be much easier if your wife/partner comes out and says she does not love you anymore and she wants to leave your marriage or partnership. What constitutes abuse in these 'instances' that are written in the previous page are the slow demoralisation of you to make you react negatively towards her. So to demoralize you, you will be provoked into leaving your home or doing something you regret. By emotionally abusing you she is trying to put the blame on you so others whoever they may be will think you are the 'bad one', you are the one who had made her do all what she is doing, When you react by shouting out your frustrations you are the 'violent one'. Even your children will be set against you as is usually the trend.

She emotionally abuses you so everyone will say it is your fault, many will ask you 'what did you do to her?' as though as the man you must have done something to her. Forgetting that women can also fall out of love with their

husbands or partners or love someone else and want to leave you after she
believes she has got what she wants and you have served your purpose.
Exactly the same way we hear men do.

She can also feel trapped in a marriage realising she had made the wrong
choice and now wants out. Also she can be suffering the effects of depression
or post-natal depression or she might have mental illness problems. All what
will not be discussed because traditionally and culturally, African women in
particular will not easily admit or accept that there are mental health issues
confronting them when emotionally abusing their husbands/partner. If your
wife cannot or will not communicate with you, if you can, find someone you
can talk to. In Britain it is difficult to talk in certain ways about what is
considered personal problems.

It is one of the aims of this book that by the time you are reading it there will
be someone and somewhere you can go to speak confidentially if you feel
you are being emotionally abused as a man and especially a Black man in
Britain and the Diaspora.

Do not fall into the trap of saying 'typical women' when all this is going on
and wrong around you. You are in a different culture and environment now
away from the one you perhaps grew up. Continue to try as much as you can
to communicate with your wife. Most importantly ask her what you have
done to make her feel and behave in the way you have noticed she is
behaving towards you. Try all you can, and if she laughs in your face and at
all your efforts, begin to admit to yourself that your marriage is beginning to
crumble but you do not need to be emotionally abused when your marriage is
crumbling.

The breakdown of any marriage/partnership is emotional and difficult.
Normally decisions to separate or divorce are not taken lightly. As it is
constantly said, 'you have to work hard at a marriage'. It is particularly
painful if you are family orientated, spent years building up your family and
loving your children, wanting to give them that sense and felling of a family
unit you perhaps never had or had and intend to continue and then watch it all
crumble before your very eyes, through no singularly direct fault of yours.

Still, love cannot be forced and one cannot force any other human being to love you. Love as most prefer to know it, is not something you can buy in a store, put on your mantel piece and cherish like an object. This is why it is important to stress the difference between the emotions of a marriage breakdown and emotional abuse. We have heard too often of an amicable separation or divorce but we know in most cases at least for one party divorce for them is not amicable.

*"It is true, however, than women tend to abuse men differently than men abuse women. Women generally favor **emotional abuse** tactics, making the abuse much more **difficult to detect.***

*Men usually are blamed for abuse because of modern gender stereotypes. Women are perceived as the weaker, gentler sex, whereas men are perceived as being stronger and having natural tendencies toward violence. **These stereotypes are false.***"

Victoria Ramos
Also read the chapter 'Coming to Terms and the Aftermath'.
And if you do not believe………
Read this;
Jeremy Kyle Defends Male Domestic Violence Victim from Laughing Audience

The Jeremy Kyle Show is a British tabloid talk show presented by Jeremy Kyle. It has been broadcast on ITV since 4 July 2005. The show is produced by ITV Studios and is broadcast each weekday. The show first appeared as a replacement for Trisha Goddard's chat show, which was moved to channel Five.

The show is based on confrontations in which guests attempt to resolve issues with others that are significant in their lives. These issues are often related to: family relationships; romantic relationships; sex drugs; and alcohol, among other issues. Frequently, guests display strong emotions such as anger and distress on the show, and Kyle is often harsh towards those that he feels have acted in morally dubious or irresponsible ways, while strongly emphasising the importance of traditional family values.

Chat showhost Jeremy Kyle, silences studio who found male guest's

experience of abuse comical. By Sophie Tighe
May 14, 2015.

Jeremy Kyle was forced to stand up for one of his guests after he admitted being the victim of domestic abuse and the audience laughed at him. The chat show host rounded on the sniggering studio as guest Geoff recalled the details of the abuse he had suffered at the hands of his ex-girlfriend, Danni.

Jeremy Kyle silenced an audience who laughed at a male victim of domestic violence [Rex] "It was violent from her side. It is a bit embarrassing to admit it," Geoff admitted, as he told the audience about an incident where Danni locked him on a balcony and he was forced to jump three stories to escape her. "I ended up in hospital and I cut all my arm and back open." The audience seemed to find the idea of a man being afraid of a violent, cheating and abusive woman comical and began to laugh before host Kyle stepped in. **"It's not funny though, is it?" he said to the audience. "I don't want to upset anyone in the audience but if a woman was sat here and a bloke had locked her in a flat and she'd been forced to jump out and injure herself you lot would not be laughing.**

"You would be saying he is a total nightmare, he should be locked up and this is disgraceful. Just because it happened to a bloke it is not funny."

While incidences of domestic violence are presumably overwhelmingly committed by men against women, there are thousands of male victims of domestic violence in the UK.

According to the ManKind Initiative, a domestic violence charity, for every three victims of domestic abuse two are female and one is male and in 2013/14 three per cent of men experienced partner abuse – that's around 500,000 men.

Do we hear enough about male victims of domestic violence? Let us find out in the comments below from replies on the internet.
Matthew a second ago

There are a lot of men out there in Britain as we speak and write who suffer crippling domestic emotional abuse from their female partner that destroys them mentally and emotionally not to talk about physical domestic violence from women to men. do not speak out, precisely because of the double standards witness on the JK show. Those audience are a cross section of the society, court, law enforcers and many others. My book on this societal manipulation and brutal injustice towards men in the 21st century is coming out soon

Read and learn of this virulent gender disease and disorder it is no laughing matter. 10 users liked this comment
Poo Shooter 40 minutes ago

Domestic violence is no joke, and the audience should be ashamed to be laughing at someone else being a victim of such. I once had a girl who fancied me attack me with a metal

bar just because I didn't want to have sex with her...so its not just men who get violence when they don't get what they want .. 1 users liked this comment
Danny 5 Minutes ago Report Abuse

It doesn't matter what gender you are, anyone can be the victim of abuse. I was the victim of mental abuse from an ex fiancée, who consistently belittled me, made me sell my stuff, and in the end left me and did so on face book. and it was my sister who told me she had changed her status. 1 Reply. 43 users liked this comment

John 1 hour 6 minutes ago Report Abuse

Men need to be men but some woman are vicious and take advantage of men's good nature (like their refusal to hit a woman). Bullies can be anyone and some women are downright monstrous! shame on the audience for laughing at this real-life issue in society. 5 Replies. 3 users liked this comment

Dean 13 minutes ago Report Abuse

*Woman are equal which means: The trouble with this vicious bit**is she needs to meet the right kind of person and feel what it like to be on the other*

end! if you dish it out you deserve it right kind of person and feel what it is like to be on the other end!. if you dish it out you deserve it back! saying:
Oleg 52 minutes ago

Daisy 59 minutes ago Report Abuse

No man and no woman has the right to lift their hands to anybody, This has been going on for many years, men will not come forward because they face ridicule about it, All domestic violence is a criminal offence, and both men and woman deserve to go to jail for it. 2 users liked this comment

Sue 31 minutes ago

Violence on either side of a relationship is not to be tolerated but if it's a woman giving the abuse it appears to be laughed at, my son had a knife to his throat by his ex wife but the police just brushed it aside however when he retaliated one day he was arrested and cautioned….

Andy 8 minutes ago

When I worked the door many years ago I found woman very much more aggressive than men in circumstance, I split a bloke and his misses up one night they were arguing reality loudly I asked them to leave. They left on the way out the chap joked with me and said "im going to pay for it…….

Steppenwolf 26 minutes ago Report Abuse

*For the record, in the workplace I have been told to fu** off*
By women and never by a man, threatened with
physical violence by women and never men
The reaction of the audience Is I think the reason why
a man is reluctant to admit violent and abuse from a
Woman. On the face of things he is bigger and stronger
and also there is reluctance for any man to hit a woman even when
provoked………

Yes!!! This was witnessed and reported in Britain.
Any Help for Men?

Yes!! But it is not as simple as that and that is the truth
A

s sense is made of the words written here, domestic abuse and domestic violence are being constantly discussed in the British Media. Advocates and campaigners speak of the need to see the

victims of domestic violence and abuse more protected and cared for and their attackers punished and brought to justice in different ingenious ways, which is advocated and supported.

Again crucially in all these programmes No man, not one British male of any ethnicity has been interviewed to give his comments on the effects of domestic violence and abuse from female to male victims. Are men scared, embarrassed to come forward and speak or have they not been invited? Yes, most definitely, men in general, are conditioned not to be weak and tell people their problems. So that's YES. Again it is easily assumed and generally accepted that men are the ones that abuse women!

When you have to deal with other isms as a Black male, is there help out there for an emotionally abused Black man? Then, the answer again is NO, there is no help for Black men in Britain and the Diaspora. Men and especially Black men are left alone, to deal with their hurt, feelings and emotional scars by this terrible abuse that is becoming increasingly prevalent, malignant and dangerous in Britain and other countries. As one article found on the internet stated 'there are virtually no shelters, programs or advocacy groups for men"

Emotional Scars

Emotional scars for men can be and are usually very deep. Not to love someone anymore is not a ticket to destroy them. From various accounts it has been revealed that many women including those from West African countries set up their husbands so brutally that they simply destabilize, debase and dislocate their husbands by framing them up to the Law. A good lawyer can advise their client on how to frame the husband up and take all that he has.
There are impossible unrealistic loopholes in the British Law for example

that can easily be charged at the unsuspecting husband. You as the husband have to be very careful not to breach any court order against you that can be taken without your consent. Even if you have done nothing wrong your wife or ex-wife can call the police at any time and tell them that you hit her or verbally abuse her and you will be arrested and in many cases charged for a false allegation.

She can build up a false case against you that she is being severely abused by you when she is not and if you are not very conversant with the law the police and inmost cases the courts will believe her. It is a terrible situation which needs addressing but so many times all the authorities are trying to back themselves up that they do not protect the truth of the man, always believing the woman to be the victim while the real victim and the one falsely accused is the man. Many stories have been told about the wife provoking and taunting the man into a reaction. Actions from a wife can be brutal, she does not have to only hit or verbally abuse the man for her to be emotionally abusing the man. There are many examples, for instance if you live in the same house and are constantly being ignored, this is also a signifier of domestic emotional abuse.

When you try to communicate you are being snubbed and when you mutter to yourself and she thinks you are verbally abusing her she can call the police and you will be arrested. Any allegation from her will have to be investigated no matter how trivial they are. It now appears for men it is a crime to cry, to wail in pain is to say you are shouting at your wife and children.

All married couples argue, should they call the police at every argument? It appears there is nothing called 'wasting police time' anymore. For many interviewed they feel it is a travesty that borders on the ridiculous. As stated earlier the system can be played by women, who are advised that they will be at an advantage.

They are effectively abusing abuse laws and depriving the real abused women to get the full attention and help that they deserve from the law. These wives and spouses are the ones actually committing a crime. Many men wrongly and falsely accused of domestic verbal or physical abuse have had their homes taken from them. They have lost everything and even been deprived of seeing their children. They go from living in two to six bedroom houses that they bought to living in a bedroom or bedsit. They are emotionally scarred for life. It never goes away the scares are still there 1 -20 years later and for life.

Many find it discriminatory and unbelievable that in this day and age when a man is falsely arrested, charged and bailed by the police, he is told not to approach his own home unless he will be arrested again then he is thrown to the streets even if the address given for bail is squalid or 30 miles away from his home, another emotional scar. There are no men's aid homes he can go in for one night or a week's shelter.

To visit his home he has to be escorted by police to collect his belongings. A shame to him for the neighbors will view him as a violent person, or a convicted person while he has in fact done no wrong, another emotional scar. When she calls your children to see you handcuffed by the police is another emotional scar. When she laughs at you when the police are taking you to their van as a criminal is another emotional scar.

There are many more. In most cases, it is the abused men who have to start again and remember with no help or support just because they are men. Your house could be taken from you over false allegations and your children taken from you for the same reasons. You will find yourself on the streets alone with very little or no help whatsoever and the alleged 'victim' enjoying the fruits of your years of labour.

She will now be in the house you bought or the house you both bought languishing in style over false allegations while you are suffering on the streets in a new strange town where you know no one, without a job and in some cases drinking and begging in the streets.
Many want to ask the British Courts and Courts in the Diapora, is it fair? Are all men monsters? Are all men abusers to be arrested at a call to the police? Should many police officers not be trained now at discretion and discernment?

Help is clearly needed urgently but many will not get help until the wrongly accused men who have suffered emotional abuse start talking loudly and clearly. Admitting you are being abused verbally, physically and especially emotionally by your wife/girlfriend/female partner does not make you less of a man.

The Courts must be helped to see the constant pattern by these women who come from specific countries disguised as wives and abuse the system over and over again to the detriment and destruction of innocent men. It should be a crime for a partner to falsely accuse their partner or ex-partner of abuse when it fact they are innocent. An allegation of abuse should not be taken lightly and must be investigated with the complainant and accuser given a custodial sentence if found guilty of false allegations.

'Another statement found states, 'A man has no right to defend himself by law against a woman' in American Law and very much the British way currently.

It seems the reality is; expect to be accused of Domestic Violence or Incident and all types of abuse from verbal abuse to financial abuse and many more abuses she, a deceitful spouse/partner can get away with. Expect to be arrested and the police to burgle your house just because she lied against you.

It is all part of the plan of deceit and playing the system. It is usually said that in most cases of marriage breakdown, the British courts will consider the child/children first, the woman/partner second the pets third and last on the list, the man.

Helping the Emotionally Abused Man
N

ot being a trained Psychologist or Clinical/Nonclinical Psychiatrist, Therapist or Counselor, this is not the platform to give expert medical advice. What is being written here are accounts of and

indications from numerous men who have healed and are still healing from domestic emotional abuse? Certainly all individuals heal in different ways and at their own pace. However one common strand that has been noticed is, domestic emotionally abused men all go through a phase of 'depression' from mild to severe. It is common for most men not to acknowledge that they are depressed or going through a depressed stage in their lives brought about by emotional abuse. Especially when depression can be used against them by their abusive spouses and crafty lawyers to take their children and home away from them.

It is well documented that marriage breakdown that leads to divorce can trigger both spouses to become depressed or have a 'meltdown', 'nervous breakdown' and ' mental breakdown'.

Recently a man in despair asked 'Who would believe me'? then went on to say 'she smiles at the neighbors when we all meet, smiles with our friends, then indoors on our own she turns into a monster, belittling me at every opportunity, telling me I should have acted in this way or that or said this or that. When I keep quite she says I am ignoring her when I try to explain myself I am arguing with her, then when she physically hits me and I dodge her blows or shield myself, she runs to the neighbors crying and call our friends crying. They now come thundering on our front door calling me all types of derogatory names and threatening to call the cops on me. I try to tell them I am not the one at fault but they are convinced by her fake tears that I am a male monster. Who would believe me? it has affected my work and everything I do'

What is not widely documented is the amount of men who go through these destructive illnesses through domestic emotional abuse. It beggars belief that when a man has been emotionally abused severely and 'pushed to the wall', when he shows any sign of strain or a meltdown this can actually be used to his detriment in the courts of law, suggesting that he is not stable and has committed some sort of 'crime'. In most cases if it was the other way round she would be viewed sympathetically and vindicated even if she is just putting on another deceitful act.
In trying to help men who have gone through or are going through this abuse 'tough love' will perhaps make their situation worse not better. Remember it has taken a man who is all macho on the outside to confide in you about his emotional abuse. Laughing it off or telling him to 'snap out of it' or 'move on'will not help and can actually get him to close up and bottle up again. In this type of emotional trauma there is no 'moving on'. The victim cannot 'move on' casually until healed and that means dealing with the pain.

Remember that his mental, psychological and emotional being has been ruptured. He has probably been put down so much, made to feel that he is useless and a failure when he is not, teased for being unemployed when his spouse is employed. Provoked to the extreme to react negatively and emotional violated. What is needed is not some 'bravado' talk from men, women and friends alike who want to help but go about this help in the wrong way.

For some taking them to night clubs and engaging them in nightlife might be the answer for others it is not. Night clubs can be the loneliest place on earth for the emotionally abused. For some the last thing they want to see are women and men dancing and enjoying themselves as this can be a poignant reminder of what their spouse had got up to when she went out clubbing and in some cases flirting with other men or the joy of clubbing you once shared together and the pain and loss all come rushing back.

Getting your emotional abused male friend, brother or cousin to engage in one night stands does not also help some men. In most cases they are not healing but on the rebound and in severe cases they end up taking all their frustrations , anger and fears on the innocent victim who just wants some 'fun'. Sex is not the answer in all cases.

Getting involved in a serious relationship quickly when coming out of a domestic emotional abusive relationship can also be difficult not only for the emotionally abused man but also for the potential partner. Diving into the deep end too quickly when not fully healed or recovered can bring up all the unfriendly vicious ghosts of the past – on the rebound again.

Pilling the emotionally abused man with drugs and alcohol constantly, in most cases will do more harm than good. This is not healing. It is finding an escape from the present, from the feelings of worthlessness and self-doubt the emotional abuser has fed the man. Many will wake up sober and seek for the drink and/or drugs again when the negative memories begin to flood in and the emotional pain starts to hurt. It can turn into a vicious circle, running away from you towards yourself. All leading to depression and mental illness.

Some men have coped by disappearing to another state, country or town. For them there is a need to leave everything behind and start again. In most cases they take on another persona, another self, usually by changing their physical appearance, growing a beard, growing long hair or shaving of their beard and long hair and this extends to a change in their wardrobe. Discarding the old self and reawakening the new self.

If you are not a trained professional in emotional and mental health the most effective way to help is to get to know who your friend, brother, cousin etc… is by being silent and listening. Remember there are very, very, very few therapist or counselors, indeed if any, trained in healing domestic emotional abuse suffered by men and again in particular Black men from African and Carribean origin who are British or American. They will probably bore you with all their pain and regret and when you have finally got him to talk about his feelings and the extent of his emotional abuse be prepared for a long repetitive soliloquy. It is a form of healing. It is important to just listen.

Also remember most men bottle up their emotions because they are trying to live up to the ever changing mythical stereotype of being 'a man' that has been lumbered on them from birth. then when they can take it no more the bottle burst and they 'snap' then trigger the button of self-destruction. This is what all are trying to avoid.

Any support group will help initially but it is difficult to find. It also helps to have many discussions, including gender and equality issues discussions, healthy and unhealthy relationships, identifying warning signals that will enable potential victims to identify when a relationship is becoming abusive. Also the effects of different types of abuse to help recognise the feelings of low esteem, self-blame and shame emotional abuse can induce.

Abuse between partners have effects on the children living with them, Staying, coping and surviving in this type of relationship can be stressful and strenuous. Try to recognise danger signals and avoid them in front of your child/children. The victim needs to know how he can leave a crushing relationship. It is important to learn why a person remains in an abusive relationship and the emotional and practical steps that can help men leave safely.
As mentioned before, it is important to note that the first barrier too help for abused men is admitting they are being abused in any form by their female wives or partner. It is well know and researched that men have been programmed not to talk, not to show any emotions whosoever and to appear

strong and protective of their homes, female wives/partners, child/children. So it is very difficult for men to talk especially men of Caribbean/African origin. These conditionings of men are the fertile breeding ground for the female emotional abuser.

The Church, Mosque Halls, and other places of worship have been known to provide some form of therapy for the emotionally abused. However it is important to note that the Pastors, Priests, Imams, Elders and other leaders in these places are also human are usually not trained counselors or therapists in this area and are perhaps quietly going through the same trauma as you. They might be able to ease your trauma but should not be expected to immediately and automatically cure and heal you. It is worth remembering that many men, and especially many women cannot comprehend the fact that a man can be emotionally abused by a woman. This belief is strongly held by some women in some African countries. Many women will simply not believe their sisters and friends are emotionally abusing their male partners/husbands or can be that vicious. Many, both male and female will ask the man seeking help 'what did you do to her'? Easily forgetting that some women can be just downright wicked, manipulative, obsessive and are out to hurt the man in their lives for money, property , greed, titles, children and many more deceitful reasons just like some men! All should try not to immediately fall into gender stereotyping and try to listen to the honesty of the emotionally abused man seeking help.

The reason these guides are being written down is not to suggest that it is easy for you as a man to get over your battered and bruised emotions, your mental, emotional and psychological abuse. It will take time and pain. This book is just one avenue to begin to find ways to heal. Many emotionally abused men have been wounded for far too long than necessary and have never really healed. As a man it is hoped you now have some information.. Your healing begins here. You are not alone.
All married or partnered couples argue. Disagreement is part of the agreement in marriage and of course how this is resolved by each individual or couple differs. There are too many images in Britain showing men shouting at women. Behind closed doors it is certain many wives and girlfriends bully and shout at their husbands and boyfriends and also physically attack them.

Situations can escalate very quickly. It will help enormously if the warning signs of domestic emotional abuse are recognized early to prevent more domestic emotional damage. You should recognize when slowly but consistently you are being put down not only during arguments. Again as written before:

* When during conversations she suddenly purposely changes the topic this makes the point of emphasizing quietly that you are not being listened to.

* When she gets angry all of a sudden and arguments are being picked out of nowhere.

* When she suddenly begins to cover her nudity from you her 'husband'. Remember it has been said, 'a woman's body is her treasure she only shares or shows it to those she treasures. (In most cases anyway).

* When you are consistently told. 'Look at your life' ,'you are not a man', 'you are useless' 'you are a failure, 'what have you archived in this country'

* When you are being compared to other man 'look at your mates, they are all successful, they have passed you and you are still here suffering'.

* When she begins to put you down in front of your friends and her friends. When she begins to demand money she knows you cannot afford, then laughs at you when you do not give her, telling you, 'you are not capable of being a good husband'.

When you are being undermined and shouted at in front of your child/ children. Contradicting all you tell them, systematically directing your child/children to disrespect you.
* When she leaves your families home with your children and you do

not know where she has gone with them especially if she knows you love your child/children and are attached to them.

* Begins to destroy what is precious to you, no matter how trivial she may call them, they are still yours and she knows you cherish them. Tries to display no emotions when lovemaking. She gives a disdainful, regretful laugh

directed at you after making love.

* Begins to go out with her family and friends without inviting you or including you in joint family away trips or parties. Also constantly refuses to go to any of your own functions, such as office functions or family events.

* Becomes all of a sudden interested in wealthy people, millionaires, and far richer lifestyles she knows both of you cannot afford. Always deliberately frowning and acting dissatisfied around you, verbally abusing you at every opportunity.

* When she begins to slowly separate herself from you by putting her clothes and belongings in a separate cupboard or room.

* When she begins to stop going to church, mosque, mass or study with you as frequently as before or in some cases begins to go to another church or place or worship with her 'friends'.

* Begins to lie constantly about everything.

All these will be going on or has gone on when you have tried as much as possible to communicate with your wife/partner and all you have got were short sharp answers, snaps, that you should 'shut up' she is tired, 'not now' statements. Not wanting to communicate at all or discuss anything with you except financially to her advantage.

So why don't these men just leave?
Why men don't leave immediately.

Many people have trouble understanding why a woman who is being abused by her husband or boyfriend doesn't simply just leave him. When the roles are reversed, and the man is the victim of the abuse, people are even more bemused. However, anyone who's been in an abusive relationship knows that it's never that simple. Ending a relationship, even an abusive one, is rarely easy.

You may feel that you have to stay in the relationship because:

You want to protect your children. You worry that if you leave your spouse will harm your children or prevent you from having access to them. Obtaining custody of children is always challenging for fathers, but even if you are confident that you can do so, you may still feel overwhelmed at the prospect of raising them alone. **You feel ashamed.** Many men feel great shame that they've been beaten down by a woman or failed in their role as protector and provider for the family. **Your religious beliefs** dictate that you stay or/and your self-worth is so low that you feel this relationship is all you deserve. **You're in denial.** Just as with female domestic violence victims, denying that there is a problem in your relationship will only prolong the abuse. **You may believe that you can help your abuser or she may have promised to change.** But change can only happen once your abuser takes full responsibility for her behavior and seeks professional counseling or treatment.

There are lack of resources for abused men. Many men have difficulty being believed by the authorities, or their abuse is minimized because they're male.

Finding support and tips on safely leaving an abusive relationship.
Domestic violence and abuse can have a serious physical and psychological impact on both you and your children. The first step to stopping the abuse is to reach out. Talk to a friend, family member, or someone else you trust.

Admitting the problem and seeking help doesn't mean you have failed as a man, father or as a husband. You are not to blame, and you are not weak. As well as offering a sense of relief and providing some much needed support, sharing details of your abuse can also be the first step in building a case against your abuser and protecting your child/children.

When dealing with your abusive partner:
Be aware of any signs that may trigger a violent response from your spouse or partner and be ready to leave quickly. If you need to stay to protect your children, call the emergency services. The police have an obligation to protect you and your children, just as they do a female victim.

Never retaliate. An abusive woman or partner will often try to provoke you into retaliating or using force to escape the situation. If you do retaliate, you'll almost certainly be the one who is arrested and/or removed from your home.

Get evidence of the abuse. Report all incidents to the police and get a copy of each police report. **Keep a journal of all abuse with a clear record of dates, times, and any witnesses.** Include a photographic record of your injuries and make sure your doctor or hospital also documents your injuries. Remember, medical personnel are unlikely to ask if a man has been a victim of domestic violence, so it's up to you to ensure the cause of your injuries are documented.

Keep a mobile phone, evidence of the abuse, and other important documents close at hand. If you and your children have to leave instantly in order to escape the abuse, you'll need to take with you evidence of the abuse and important documents, such as passport and driver's license. It may be safer to keep these items outside of the home.

Obtain advice from a domestic violence program or legal aid resource about getting a restraining order or order of protection against your spouse and, if necessary, seeking temporary custody of your children. As a man you too can do these too don't think you can't!

*In an emergency call 999, 911 or the emergency lines in your country. If as a Man you are being physically or verbally abused in any way whatsoever; CALL THE POLICE.
*** YOU TOO CAN CALL THE POLICE**

As said over and over again, for most suffering from domestic emotional abuse and especially for MEN the greatest barrier into coming to recognise this type of abuse is **Denial**.

Most men will always think that they can 'fix things' in their marriage and relationships and make 'things better' when they are clearly victims. It has to be understood that emotions are not objects that can be easily fixed.

The first hurdle is to recognize that you are actually a victim and report it. You have to be aware of the patterns and begin to record them. Do not brush them away, they will only get worse. Do not be ashamed or afraid to report them to the police. Go to the police or call the police and tell them of your fears and concerns. Now they cannot fine you for wasting police time which is what many men think will happen. Speak to the police clearly if you think you are being 'set up' for your spouse to lay claim to your property, properties or to give an edge to divorce proceedings.

Living with emotional or physical abuse can take its toll on your health and general well-being. Take care of yourself and find healthy ways to deal with the stress of an abusive marriage, relationship or partnership. Eat healthy foods and try to get enough rest. Remind yourself of your unique qualities and talents. Indulge in a hobby or interest you enjoy. Try starting an exercise routine or reading a good book to escape for a while.

Keep your support system strong. Try to maintain your relationships with friends and family as much as you can. Your wife/girlfriend may try to limit the amount of time you spend with others or sabotage your friendships. Tell them what is going on so they will understand if they don't hear from you as often or as regularly as before so they can act quickly when you call for help in a emergency.

Learn about the dynamics of emotional abusive relationships. Knowing more about the pattern of abuse will help you understand that the abuse is not your fault but is something your wife/girlfriend chooses to do.

Set some boundaries with your partner. When she starts a verbal tirade, do not engage and try to match her abuse. Psychologist Marie HartwellWalker's article "Signs You Are Verbally Abused: Part II," published on the Psych Central website, suggests calmly letting her know that you are sorry she feels that way, but that you expect her to treat you with respect. If she continues, simply walk out of the room. However this will perhaps not always be easy as she could follow you around the home or place with more verbal abuse.

Prepare a safety plan. The National Domestic Violence Hotline stresses the importance of developing a practical, personalized plan to stay safe while in an abusive relationship, when leaving an abuser or after the relationship is over. Even if your partner as never been physically violent, verbal and emotional abuse can quickly escalate to physical abuse. Your plan should include identifying safe areas of your home and planning an escape route. You should keep a phone with you at all times and know who you can call for help. Create a code word or signal so trusted friends and neighbours know if you need emergency assistance. Do not think you do not need to because you are a man. Try not to be embarrassed to speak out.

Start looking for a good Solicitor if you can afford one. Remember you can be in denial to think she will not take your 'disagreement' this far. You might be wrong, you do not know, so protect yourself by speaking to a solicitor. If you cannot afford a solicitor and cannot get legal aid begin to go to support groups like Fathers for Justice or Family needs Fathers etc.... and they can help you with legal advice. These groups are for all Fathers regardless of race.

Never lie to the police, shout or contradict the police. Remember in most cases, they need to get the facts, do not give them any reason to arrest you and be accused of resisting arrest or aggression. Let them do their job. Yours is to stay calm and rational.

Go to the citizen's advice bureau and find out all the Court Orders that can be served against you even if you are innocent. Another big barrier is not knowing what can be used against you by the law, so many men are not prepared and do not safe guard themselves appropriately.
When a call is made out to the police of an allegation even if false, you will be handcuffed and arrested, you will be read your rights and led into a police van or car. Never resist arrest. The police are just doing their job and do not know the circumstances of your situation. They have just been called to go to an address and arrest the alleged accused. Yes it would be humiliating and you will feel embarrassed, if you are innocent look at the bigger picture and hopefully in future you will be able to call a Charity (in progress) and a few others to guide you through the process.

When in the police station you will be searched and your belongings taken, your fingerprints and photographs taken then you will be locked in a police cell and left there for as long as it takes to do the paper work on your case. The police cell is not nice, if you are not used to being on your own you will find it very hard and frustrating. This is easier said than done when your emotions are running high and you are frightened, but try and remain calm and focus on the events that can calm you and take your mind off your present environment.

When you are eventually interviewed after being in the police cell for up to 12 to 24 hours or more, always insist on having a solicitor in your interview, it is your right and it is free. Do not think you do not need one because you want it over and quickly so you can go home. Get one, remember you cannot fix this alone and without help.

Unless you have been otherwise informed NEVER agree or accept a POLICE CAUTION. It is not a conviction but it will come up on an enhanced CRB check and this could affect you career seriously. Again it is worth noting that at present in British law your wife/girlfriend can call the police for you at any time, for any reason and you will be arrested even if you are innocent. This cannot be emphasized enough. Apparently at present to the law of the land in Britain, remember you are a MAN and for that reason you are to blame and everyone will blame you. You are guilty until proven innocent, not the other way round. The experience will leave you traumatised. For some, you will be traumatized for days, weeks, months and years especially if you are innocent. Know what an ARREST is, a CAUTION, a CONVICTION, a MOLESTATION, RESTRICTION and OCCUPATION ORDER, POLICE PROTECTION ORDER ETC.. This is important so you know what can be used against you.

Someone once said, 'to be a man you have to learn how to cry'. This is true. Do not be ashamed to cry in front of anyone, you are not less of a man you are a human being showing emotions and that means you are STRONG.

Afterwards if you feel sadden by the constant belittling and name calling. Remember only small people make other people feel small in order for them to feel big. This is not your bag, you are better than that; you are strong by not retaliating, show control by not responding in kind, show moral backbone because it takes a strong, intelligent and exceptional man to hold back as long as you did. If you get upset, sad and humiliated, it shows you are human. Get help and get support no matter how small it may seem.

What is perhaps stopping you from reaching out for help is this fear of being considered a wimp or weak and that makes many men reluctant to call the police for their wives or girlfriends?. Many men have asked themselves numerous times why did they not call the police when their wives/girlfriends were being physically, and verbally abusive towards them? What is it that made them not make that call when their spouse will not hesitate to make the call to the police? There is the fear that once the police is involved, the authorities are notified and there are the issues of work and your workplace being notified, feeling guilty when you are not guilty and the stigma of a police case if you are a Black man

What is this psychological barrier and where does it stem from? There is a history and fear of the authorities, stereotyping, prejudice, discrimination, Stop and Search, disproportionality of Black men arrested, detained, in prisons, in psychiatric hospitals. So this is why most men are reluctant to report their spouses or implicate their spouses while their spouses are not reluctant to throw them in jail? For many Black men in Britain and the Diaspora, this dilemma contains a lot of cultural ramifications, there needs to be some cultural context. Sometimes, whatever happens at your family home thousands of miles away may have serious implication in your home country when families do get involve; yours and hers.
Cultural values and instincts may dictate or inclines you to protect your family name, her and your child/children if you have any, while in reality she does not need protection from you; she has the police and the authorities. Anger and frustration, does all things and men speak of their spouse spitting on them and they do nothing, kicking them and they do nothing, pushing and shoving and verbal abuse from partners becomes common place to them that they almost expect it to happen all the time.

Too many times it is heard 'you are a man, just walk away', many forgetting that when you are being emotionally stabbed repeatedly it is not easy to 'just walk away' in fact in most cases it is more harmful to just walk away, for all is again bottled in waiting to explode. When most men reply they fear they may get arrested for verbal and other abuse. Even when you defend yourself from her blows and her verbal abuse you might still be arrested and accused if she calls the police. Sometimes men do not want to take that chance. So they take it and take it which is eventually emotionally destructive.

For too long men have suffered in silence trying to hold on to the stereotypical notion of what constitutes 'a man'. That does not work anymore in Britain and the Diaspora. Pick up the phone and call the police if your spouse begins to emotionally abuse you. It will be recorded and will work to your advantage when it gets worse. Do not be afraid, do not be ashamed, and do not be shy. Call! If you do not call the police she will and it will be to your detriment.

If you are charged and summoned to go to court be prepared for; **Your Hearing. Day/s in Court.**

Like hundreds of thousands of Men and Black Men in the Diaspora, who would have never attended a court trial or hearing and do not know how the Court system works, you would naturally be terrified of attending court when you have been falsely accused or charged and summoned to attend. Before attending you have to be prepared. However there are a few facts to be aware of:

According to various testimonies, first you are a Man, second if you are Black. Both put together you are a lethal cocktail of negative perception, perceived as such by almost everyone in the building. This natural combination of humanity in nature, you cannot help, but that as you will be told, is your problem.
This is not drastic. When you check all the statistics in Britain's prisons, mental institutions, police cells, use of tasers and arrests, people that look like Black men are over represented. This is no accident but you are seen as an accident waiting to happen. With that in mind you have to compose yourself.

Don't be deflated, lose confidence or give up, just be aware of how you are perceived and this will help on how you can prove your innocence.

Remember the district Judge or magistrate does not know you and a lot of bad eggs must have passed under her judgment (in the family courts it is usually a female judge) so feelings and reactions are on how you present yourself or how you are presented.

Most men are shocked that they are being presented in front of a judge on what might appear to them as minimal, flimsy unimportant charges, when there are more serious cases to be solved, but the legal system has a duty of care to prevent presumed harm, so although you know the truth you will be treated tried and judged as a criminal. Your spouse or ex – spouse in most cases will lie against you even after taken an oath on any holy book and you

will find yourself asking, 'what is going on'? All forms of excuses and
emotional blackmail will be used. If she has a lawyer and you don't and you
are not conversant with legal language you will be at a disadvantage so
prepare and ask questions before you appear in court. If you can afford it get
a Lawyer In the case of divorce, restraining, molestation, occupation and
other orders you will find they can go on for 1 -3 years even more if you do
not bother to stop them. Remember you can appeal against any order if you
think it is unfair. You fill in a form and apply, there is usually a cost attached
to it. However it can take 3 to 4 months before the case is listed for hearing
by which time your order might have been lifted. If your order is longer it is
worth appealing.

Get all your documents ready. Your solicitor might prepare what is called a
Bundle which is a file of charges and evidence. If you do not have a solicitor,
go with your own notes. Rehearse all what you have written down and make
it all clear. Make sure you are on time to court. Being late does not speak
well of your character. On trial and when you are cross examined be calm; do
not show your frustrations or your anger at the lies against you. Lawyers will
always support their clients because they are being paid to do so. They will
have no sympathy for you and will use all they can to make you look like the
guilty villain you are not so as to confuse the judge. State and present your
case clearly and rationally, cry if you must, it is not against the law it is better
than banging your fist on the desk in frustration which will be seen as
violence.

Many have said the entire family court system in Britain for example is
biased towards women that is why so many toxic fraudulent women
capitalize on this and are bold to go to court with false and flimsy allegations.
It has been noted that 95% of the time the female can get away with anything
in the family court and she will cry if she needs to for that extra effect to win
the judge over. That does not mean you can never win. If you are innocent let
it be seen. There are some judges and magistrates in the system that knows of
the deceit that can go on from female domestic emotional abusers but they
are very rear.

Going in and out of court is not easy and is emotionally draining, remember
you are already suffering from emotional abuse and this can be another strand

of the abuse. You could develop anxiety, fall depressed and give up easily, there might be sleepless nights and fear of the system you think unjust and seeing your abuser again.

Remember that the court process takes time and it is fair to say in most cases the courts are understaffed, overstretched and sometimes cannot cope with the amount of cases they have to deal with. Meanwhile you are a statistic and will be asked to wait for months before the next hearing, listing or trial. It is this waiting period that can affect your health and emotional well-being. Without help and support you can be even more isolated than before. This can be worse if your abuser is not allowing you to see your children and you have been told by the courts not to go to your home.

It can appear easier said than done but at this time try to be resilient. Do something like sport, take frequent walks, speak to family, friends, your support group and if you have none of these join a gym, activity in your local library and if in employment try as much as you can to concentrate on your work with the help of colleagues who understand. Don't think this cannot affect your job performance, it can and if possible speak to someone in your workplace about your current situation.
Try to always look good, dress well. In such situations it is easy to let yourself go. Stay focused and think about your positive goals like getting on with your life again after court by planning your future and things you will do once it is all over.

When the day finally arrives for your trail or hearing, if you do not have a lawyer go with someone to court to give you moral and emotional support. A close friend or a family member.

Coming to Terms and the Aftermath
B

y now you should be able to listen to yourself and your inner voice which you have ignored for so long. If your inner voice now begins to speak to you again and tells you to run in the other direction, tells you

that you are being treated unkindly and bullied again and you feel something is wrong, this time listen and run in the other direction.

Yes, you the victim will feel like a fool, stupid, used financially, emotionally abused then discarded and the wounding words that were and in some cases still being used to hurt you with many other poisoned words that has been thrown at you and that you will throw at yourself. Worst still, you will think that your partner has won, has outsmarted you with her lies and deceit, it will hurt even more if you are innocent. Do not run away from your feelings confront them. In the full light of day, it can happen to anyone, it just happened to be you now. Do not let this period define you and do not let your life be dictated by this period.

No one has won anything, not you, not her, and not the children, if you have any. The fact is you have all lost especially if children are involved they are the biggest loser in all this because none of it was their fault and in some cases it can be seen as very irresponsible and damaging on the part of the parents to use the child or children as bait to get to each other. The children's mental health will be affected the longer they witness their parents undergoing these struggles and it can mark them negatively through their adult lives, if they don't get help.

Bitterness, regret, anger, frustration, the pain of the injustice in the justice system, the manipulations and all the emotions that separation and divorce comes with will pass through you. Try not to let them reside in you for long let them pass. Again as a man you will want to bottle it all up. There is no shortcut, but there can be light at the end of the tunnel. You have to face the problem squarely, you do not have to do it alone and it will be painful but you will begin at some point to heal and grow again though it might be long and painful.

Try to think! What do I do now? Where do I go from here, what was I before I got involved as a partner or husband with this person? What were and are my achievements? Anything you consider your achievements even if others might disregard them write them down. Remember if you have been emotionally abused as a man, you have been put down, disregarded, you have not been encouraged in anything that you have done or tried to do so don't look away and think that was not an achievement because the person you were with did not see it. If it meant something to you write it down. If you have the means to travel, travel, get away from your immediate surroundings and people you once knew together as a couple whom would have begun to avoid you by now. Some of the friends both of you once shared might find it difficult to take sides and will not want their loyalty misunderstood by either party, others might be just downright biased, ignorant and believe that the man is always to blame. Others might just want to believe you are at fault because of their racism , prejudice and jealousy.

No one but you can determine the type of man you are or want to be. Only you can do that! Never ever sacrifice your self-esteem, your value and your worth for someone especially your partner/wife who does not respect you emotionally abuses you and treats you unkindly especially when you respect or have respected her and treat or have treated her kindly. The only person you have to prove anything to that you are a man is you and anyone around you who encourages and challenges you positively to attain your potential.

For those who have a child or children you might be surprised to find that there are nearly 2.9 million lone women parents with dependent children in Britain for example as of 2018/19 and this figure has grown from 1.9 million since 2004. Evidence will show that most of these women in Britain who intentionally make themselves single by bringing false accusations and allegations against their partners/husbands are doing so because of the benefits and property the government will dole out to them as 'abused'single mothers when they have not been abused. A highly respected family therapist and facilitator of training and support groups working with Black women and men in Britain, noted how it has been witnessed firsthand that so many Black men attempt to establish a loving relationship with their child/children only to have the door, and access to their children slam firmly shut in their faces.

Many women in this emotionally selfish and degrading cycle later admit that 'yes', I kept my children from their father and it did not help me or the children positively in fact I was wrong' Owing to this strand of greed an alarming amount of children especially Black British children are also being emotionally abused and effectively destroyed psychologically and psycho socially by their custodial usually female lone parent. So it is in effect no coincidence that they are at risk of being socially and educationally excluded and the seeds of mental health issues visit their homes and the gardens of their minds at an early age.

What is particularly sad about this is the innocuous, destructive war waged against the innocent child/children. By putting your child/children against their father these mothers are also the perpetrators of the societal ills that fuels discrimination and racism against themselves and especially Black men and youths in a society that is trying to rid itself of these internally negative labels.

This is the time you should notice the damaging effects of either of you getting revenge against each other at the children's expense. Children are often used as pawn for emotional abuse especially against men. When later in life adult children learn that their mothers were the actual reasons that their fathers were not in their lives at that crucial time when they were forming into adults, in more cases than not they become resentful and rebellious first towards their mothers then towards any authority and ultimately towards the society and community they believe has let them down. Unfortunately many mothers guilty of this deceitful tact are able to effectively hide this dishonest trait against many men, manipulating the authorities (already presumed biased) under a pretense of innocence faking victimisation from the father, projecting themselves as the helpless victim of abuse to the public and the police, as the one who is caring for their children without the help and support of the father but in private she is the manipulative merciless emotional abuser purposely and effectively keeping the father from his children whom she knows he loves and cares for.

You might find your ex partner/wife, consciously or unconsciously practicing the out of sight is the out of mind strategy. By doing so she will not have to constantly confront her guilt of rejecting and emotionally abusing you. This will begin to allow her to believe her lies and fantasies that it was all your fault when you and her know that it was not your fault. She needs to believe her lies for it makes it easier for her conscience. The fact remain that there are there are many situations where most men have actually done nothing wrong to their ex-wives/partners.
Try to deal with the negative effects of jealousy and revenge. Go and think deeply where these negative emotions might have stemmed from either from you or from her during the course of you relationship. You will be surprised to find that yes your ex partner/wife who has put you down so mercilessly and brutally has been jealous and envious of you all this while and that is

how her emotional abuse towards you has seeped in, silently, quietly and dangerously.

This is a time for your personal growth and reflection. You might have to deal with the knowledge or presence of the new man in her life. Yes it will hurt; yes it is not easy but you can deal with it, you must one way or the other, to maintain your sanity and know that you are you. What you are now and what you are yet to be without the hurt and the emotional abuse of your ex- spouse.

Be rational, this is different from being emotional. If you believe you tried all you can then do not compromise. Remember at this time you have to try to be strong and be true to yourself. Also remember that your child/children having witnessed their mother emotionally abuse you has definitely had an impact on them. Your child/ children, if you have any, no matter what sex will learn to devalue men and their vital role in a family. They will learn that it is OK to bully, yell, intimidate and emotionally abuse others. Remember 'If a man is abused he has nothing'. It is easily turned around to make him look like the abuser.

The Passive Aggressive deliberate behaviour is a well-rehearsed trait of the highly manipulative lying domestic emotional abuser. With words, you will hear words like 'you get so upset easily' 'I did not mean it that way' (having used the same words to put you down but said in a different order) and many more spiteful behavior dispensed without words, always frowning when you are around and ignoring your very existence privately and publicly. This is particularly more spiteful when it is done in front of your child/children even during visitations.

Unfortunately the stereotype of the 'bad dad' is so powerful in Britain and the Diaspora especially in African and Caribbean communities living in Britain. So when others in your neighborhood and your former joint friends notice your absence from your child/children as a caring father you are known to be, it is easy for their mother to play into the stereotype by saying you as a father 'just gave up' caring for your child/children, or that you have neglected 'them', met 'another' woman and many other lies to remove suspicion of them as wicked and manipulative. It is so easy for her to be believed by many as the stereotype of 'bad dad' has now become a virulent cancer in the

Diaspora.

The fact that the mother of your child/children, your ex-spouse/partner constantly interrupts telephone calls to your children, cancels visitation times to visit and begins to dictate the rules and regulations of when you should see your children and when not, continues your emotional abuse and extends to emotional trauma. Even if and when you have got a Court Order for visitation rights with times and dates, many spiteful mothers have been known to still flaunt the Order and determine when and if she will allow you see your child/children. The courts are still very slow to act to bring this type emotional abusive behaviour towards you and your child/children from the mother to justice.

This game of manipulation, deceit and spite, leads caring fathers and men to be arrested and jailed after attempting to see their child/children and bursting with the frustration of all his love for his child/children and the apparent loss of their love, leads many men to snap and break the vicious and some have said racists molestation orders of the courts which are now dished out indiscriminately to innocent fathers with ease. This is not particularly fair and can seem very biased especially when she has lied to the courts that the child/children you love deeply and dearly are 'scared' of you.

This pathetic game of cat and mouse, cock and bull is further domestic emotional abuse not just of you alone now but also for your child/children. It is just hoped that the courts will see all this emotional brutality for what it is and begin to take action to address and reform the current outdated and unreformed family laws and its flaws, blatantly flaunted and manipulated by these vulture like emotionally abusive spouses. This is the reality you will have to face and come to terms with. Even after the trauma of divorce and the loss of almost all you have worked for over years a condition many men affected by this inner pain find difficult to address or speak about. A condition many men who have not been through it, will rarely understand. In some cases you will have to confront the bitter truth and come to terms that your ex-wife/partner never really loved you, she just used you to come abroad or to get her 'papers' sometimes by having a child/children for you or she no longer loves you. She simply fell out of love. No matter the circumstances no man (or woman) should suffer domestic emotional abuse.

Therapy for men and especially Black men going through or damaged by divorce trauma ,child/children alienation and domestic emotional abuse is still in it's infancy and almost no-existent worldwide. It is only hoped that more work will be done in future to address and study these areas.

Moving on from an abusive relationship
* After the trauma of an abusive relationship, it can take a while to get over the pain and bad memories. It is not easy to move on * Try to work on yourself and build your confidence and self-esteem and you will get better if you work at it. It will be difficult * Even if you're eager to jump into a new relationship for support you've been missing, it's wise to take things slowly.

* Make sure you're aware of any red flag behaviour in a potential new partner ,being open and honest is the only way to build a healthy new relationship Be kind to yourself, be calm, and be rational. You are not weak. You are not alone. Help is within reach.

Don't think you do not need to talk or do not need any help.
Here and There
Here (Britain) and There (Nigeria)
H

ere in Britain and **There** 'Back Home' the stereotypical roles of husband and wife takes on different dimensions. While in some communities, **there** to be a wife is sacred and cannot be dissolved

easily, here in most communities, marriage is not a big deal and can easily be dissolved. **There** it can seem the interwoven support structure is family and community, **here** it can seem the interwoven support structure is the television, soap operas and the courts of law.

It is helpful to understand the many differences in attitudes between **here** and **there** as it is helpful to find out the deep end and shallow end of a swimming pool before diving in to swim. In order words it is easier and helpful to find out about the cultural fabric of any country when residing in it.

Here , British Men from African / Caribbean Origin would be advised to shed of the alpha dominant male position of thinking that they have to have money and give their wives money for the sole reason of thinking by giving money, she has to cook for him every time and not say no to his sexual advances anytime because he gives her money and buys her expensive gifts. **There** it might be normal and affordable. **Here** the cooking and the household chores will more likely than not have to be shared and sometimes mostly done by the man. The mind-set will in most cases have to be reset.

Here , your husband does not have to be the sole breadwinner in the household as is usually the case **there**. £100 – £1000 pounds here is not as easy to come by as the same amount in the currency **there**.

Here , do not expect your husband to pay all the bills and also give you money to maintain yourself endlessly. It is not his sole 'responsibility' as it is viewed and expected **there**.

Here , you are also meant to get a job and contribute to the bills and the contents of the household because **here** it is a collective effort between husband and wife. Financial contributions to your home should be balanced if not equal.
Within context and if you are not in the import and export business, goods and accessories are not cheap or cheaper **here** as compared to over **there** especially if you now live **here**.

Wanting all the latest gadgets, iPhone, iPods, iPads many expensive toys and credit cards readily available **here** on a pay as you go account instantly, without careful financial planning is not advisable. Easy offers could cost more later.

Here , it is difficult for a qualified Black Man and more difficult for a highly qualified Black man to get a good job or to have 'connections'. This is because there is discrimination here and though illegal many men have testified it is widely practiced. It's not because he is not 'sharp' or 'lazy'. If your spouse is hardworking and responsible he will always be on the lookout for a better job more befitting of his qualifications.

Unlike **there**, not everyone wants to be a millionaire businessman instantly. **Here**. It is not easy to go into business here as it is there with no business plan.

Here , unlike **there** it is not easy to just open a shop or hairdressing salon and start doing business instantly. It is better to avoid the trap of putting yourself under pressure to send money 'home' and to buy all sorts of unnecessary cheap merchandise to send to family and friends **there**. Ensure your priorities are not misplaced, concentrate on building up your home **here** if you have come to live here as a spouse before immediately sending money back home to buy you and your family land and build your house.

Here , spending money lavishly and showing off your wealth and riches, when you do not live on the same street or district as the rich, is viewed as vulgar, criminal and fraudulent while **there** you might be viewed as an inspiration and given respect. Unless of course, you are obviously rich and living among the rich and wealthy.

Try to integrate into the country you have come to live in, which you will become a citizen and if desired will have a child or children. **Here**, there are many topics of the day that has been of great concern to the nation for many years. Issues such as Racism, Homophobia, Xenophobia, Alcohol and Drugs Abuse, Rehab, NEET, Gender, Transgender, Anti-Semitism, the EDL, UKIP and all the current political parties and many more.
Here, Carpenters, Plumbers, Electricians, Motor Mechanics, Butchers, Fish Mongers are averagely and sometimes very wealthy individuals. Professions that are usually associated with the uneducated poor artisans **there**.

It will also help to understand the cultural practices **here**, such as Museums, National Museums, Art Galleries, Theatre's, Opera Houses, Symphony Orchestras, Proms, Notting Hill Carnival. The British Asian Festivals and many more. If you cannot visit any of these places or take part in any, it is worth finding out what they are and why they exist and why they are so important **here**.

Your life **here** is the reality, not all the fantasy of the West, going abroad and the colonial mentality fed to many before independence and still being fed to many **there**.

Here, you are encouraged to communicate and share your thoughts and ideas with your spouse. Talk together to work together.

Here you have not 'tried' for your husband because you have had one, two or more children together as husband and wife. **Here** they are his and your children too and both of you have equal parenting rights. Comments like 'I carried the child for 9 months' and 'I gave birth to the child so I can do what I like with the child' might have some resonance **there** but are redundant and irrelevant **here** and in some cases such attitudes can lead to child abuse **here**.

Do not fall into the trap of trying to go into fraud and crime to impress any woman or women friends with ill-gotten money. When caught those women you tried to impress would not visit you in prison and will most probably move on to befriend another person and you will still be in jail. Do not get caught up in the false delusion that if you are the man you have to provide money for your wife and children on tap anytime and every time.

Do not think you will begin to smell foul because your wife earns more than you. You are in a different country now and 'things', yes 'things' work differently **here**. You and your wife are expected to contribute 50/50 towards all you both do and it is very possible that one day your wife will earn more than you. Concentrate on being a good hardworking Citizen.
In general the view **here** is that a man does not always have to give you money, spend and lavish money on you for him to love you and you do not have to convince yourself that you love him because he is spending (sometimes ill-gotten) money on you. That is not love that is the man buying your complete physical affections with money and you being dishonest with your physical private self, affections and your soul because of greed and misplaced needs.

Again in general the view **there** is that comfort is attached to money and the giving of your physical self to a man or men who give you money is 'normal' and the exchange is accepted for the need to 'get on' and 'survive'.

It is too easy to dismiss these attitudes **here** and **there** as being either backward or overly liberated. It makes more sense for all to understand the cultural frameworks and traditions these views stem from and that cultural traditions on both sides have to be respected.

'The RSC's (Royal Shakespeare Company) artistic director, Gregory Doran said: "I profoundly believe we foster deeper understanding between cultures by sharing and telling each other our stories".

The **here** and **there** series will be adjusted to fit into the particular cultural differences related to the countries in the Diaspora. For example between Pakistan and America, India and Britain, Nigeria and Britain etc…. pointing out the cultural facts of **Here** and **There**.

These are just a few observations there are many more. Many will be amazed at the strong cultural views held by many even now in the digital globalised age of the 21st Century. There are certain mentalities that will be difficult for many to understand. Including the authorities. Presenting them will be helpful for all.

Also read the Chapter, 'Earning Power and Cultural Conflict'.
Looking Forward
A

s mentioned earlier it is the wish of many men and organisations to begin a charity that will help Men understand and recognise domestic emotional abuse and act swiftly to seek help.

It is evident that various organisations would particularly, like to hear from men from African communities living in the Diaspora, who have been reluctant to seek help due to cultural and other social barriers or reasons. Their experience will help others and they can also find support.

The proposed charity will also understand why men are reluctant to come forward to report abuse and address this barrier through having a place where men can come to talk in confidence with help offered to victims of this type of abuse. Sharing together and talking together to gain strength, understanding and healing to come out and to seek more direct help and advice is much needed. There is always a need to speak with someone who has gone through or is currently going through domestic emotional abuse from their wives or partner for support of one another and advice the authorities where necessary.

There are still no men refuge house/unit in Britain for example. Recently, Sweden has opened a large unit for abused men. Similarly in Sweden, trouble is brewing "Therefore, in the most 'equal' country in the world, Swedish men and fathers are, by law, second class citizens.and parents and are less worthy of protection when they suffer from domestic violence".

Previously there were no shelters for abused men in Sweden. There were however more than 250 shelters for women which are run by various branches of the mammoth organization called Riks organisationenförkvinnojourer Ochtjejjourer i Sverige (ROKS), an organization that has thoroughly been infiltrated in the Swedish government and all political parties through which they get close to unlimited state funds.

Just like in any other country in Europe and America, fathers have no say when it comes to abortions or adoptions. But in Sweden, by law, fathers have little or no say when it comes to being a father. Not to mention that women who give birth get extra money from the state simply for giving birth, regardless of whether they take care of their offspring.
And here is the alarming statistics: In Sweden 80 percent of the homeless people are men; Men are two and half times more likely to commit suicide than women in Sweden. (a 25% larger suicide rate than Romania and USA and 50% larger than India);For example there are roughly 5100 men in Swedish prisons to almost 300 women which is the most disproportionate inmates number by gender in Europe and an obvious proof of leniency propensity on the behalf of the prosecutors and judges when it comes to female criminals; "400,000 children (four hundred thousand in a 9.5 million overall population) hardly ever or never get to see their father."

The situation for men and Black men living in the Diasporas is also deteriorating to this point. There has to be a pragmatic way to move ahead and find solutions for men suffering in silence. So a place like a refuge and shelter for men who find themselves being 'kicked out' from their home, with nowhere to go and no support is much needed. It is myth to especially think all Black men have a wide circle of friends that can take them in. When the falsely accused emotionally abused male victims have nowhere to go it will be helpful to have a refuge shelter where they can go for an affordable amount for a short stay or months to prepare their case for the courts and to access the type of support real abused women can easily access. Men are usually ashamed to beg for a bed or sofa as again others will think the domestic incident or violence was their fault.

Remember again that most men who have suffered emotional domestic abuse and have been refused entry to their home by the courts are usually displaced, dislocated, destabilized, disassociated and rendered homeless through no fault of their own. Most have been manipulated and lied against. If you are a man, and a Black man, you more likely to be seen as a perpetrator than the victim in the eyes of the authorities and most members of the community.

Progress is needed to begin to eradicate and heal this silent mental and emotional deterioration of innocent men. Speaking to several men conversations strongly suggests that one of the factors that have led many men in the last 15 years between the ages of 19 - 65 who have committed suicide did so owing to the added effects of domestic emotional abuse towards them, which includes the feeling of not being able to provide when they become unemployed through no fault of theirs and being blamed for it, prevented from seeing their child/children, losing their homes and many more. However the stereotypical psychological barriers being heaped on many men have prevented them from mentioning their emotional abuse earlier, or indeed adding it to their suicide note, if any. So we are not able to know for sure but the indicators are very high.

Protect yourself

This book is about awareness and a help guide for all men who have been, still are and are venerable to be victims of domestic emotional abuse, false allegations of domestic violence and abuse from their wives, girlfriends or female partners. It does not have all the answers but should help to address some of the process of what constitutes emotional abuse and help to navigate the blurred lines to find a way to get help and justice.

Just like the 'Me too' movement, it is worth starting a movement for men to take a stand against these deceitful women. Men should gather the courage to talk and show solidarity and courage to admit domestic emotional abuse to each other and others that have been through these deceit as well and just like 'Me too' to say to the world **'As well'.**

Do not suffer in silence, Help is rear for men but please talk to those who